SPECTRE GUNNER

SPECTRE GUNNER

The AC-130 Gunship

MSGT. DAVID M. BURNS

iUniverse, Inc.
Bloomington

Spectre Gunner
The AC-130 Gunship

iUniverse books may be ordered through booksellers or by contacting:

iUniverse
1663 Liberty Drive
Bloomington, IN 47403
www.iuniverse.com
1-800-Authors (1-800-288-4677)

ISBN: 978-1-4759-6972-6 (sc)
ISBN: 978-1-4759-6974-0 (hc)
ISBN: 978-1-4759-6973-3 (ebk)

Library of Congress Control Number: 2013900056

Printed in the United States of America

iUniverse rev. date: 01/28/2013

This book is dedicated to the Spectre crewmembers who lost their lives in defense of their country. Each and every one of them was a very special airman whom the nation can be very proud of. It is also dedicated to all the Spectre men—past, present, and future—who are still living up to the standards of duty, honor, and country in their everyday lives. And to the Spectre airmen who are now involved in another war.

Special dedication to Senior Master Sergeant Brian P. Morrison, who took care of me in the worst of times and always kept his word; to Chief Master Sergeant P. J. Cook, a gunner who helped me with parts of this book; and to all the Spectre men who have passed away since the end of the Vietnam War. I love them and miss them all very much, and I look forward to seeing them again someday—but not too soon, I hope. They actually lived the code: duty, honor, country.

Contents

GLOSSARY

AAA (Triple A): anti-aircraft artillery
ABCCC: Airborne Command and Control Center
AC: aircraft commander
ACM: additional crew member
AP: air police
ARRS: air rescue and recovery service
ARVN: Army of the Republic of Vietnam
BC: Black Crow
BDA: battle-damage assessment
Charlie: vietcong
DMZ: demilitarized zone
E&E: escape and evade
Fence: border between Thailand and Laos
fire base: army artillery base
FIS: fighter intercepter squadron
fragged: assigned to a specific area of operations
TFS: tactical fighter squadron
Gomer: NVA Vietcong, and communist troops
ground-pounder: a non-flying airman
IO: illuminator operator
IR: infrared operator
Jolly Green: air force rescue personnel flying HH-53 helicopters
LLTV: low-light-level TV
mm: millimeter
Moonbeam: nighttime call sign for ABCCC
NKP: nakhon phanom
NOD: night-observation device

Palace Gun: special air force volunteer program, aerial gunner
PJ: Para rescueman
SAM: surface-to-air missile
sparkle: firing tracers into the target so the F-4 can see where to bomb
TDY: temporary duty
TIC: troops in contact
winchester: out of ammunition

P R E F A C E

Prior to joining the US Air Force in 1967, I joined the US Navy when I was fifteen years old. I spent sixteen years in the US Navy as an aviation ordnance man (airborne weapons). My last duty station was at the US Navy Recruit Training Command in San Diego, California, where I trained new recruits for three years. In 1969, I was assigned to the Sixteenth Special Operations Squadron as an aerial gunner. After retiring in 1978, I wanted to write a book about my experiences in the squadron, but I kept putting it off. In 2012, I decided to tell the story of the most outstanding men I have ever had the privilege to know. It is a story of a select group of men who chose to fly very hazardous nightly combat missions over uncharted mountainous terrain deep in enemy territory called the Ho Chi Minh Trail. These men were shot at nightly; in six cases, they were shot down. Bravery, honor, and heartbreak were nightly occurrences.

David M. Burns
Master Sergeant, US Air Force, Retired

SPECTRE GUNNER

My story begins in December 1969. I had just completed aerial gunners' school in Lockbourne, Ohio. I attended survival school at Fairchild Air Force Base in Washington and finished at the Pacific Air Forces (PACAF) Jungle Survival School in the Philippines.

I was assigned to the Sixteenth Special Operations Squadron as an aerial gunner in the "Palace Gun" program. I was part of a twenty-six-man replacement (both officers and enlisted) crew that was replacing squadron members who had finished their one-year tours.

I knew the first sergeant of the combat wing at Clark Air Base since I had served a previous Vietnam tour in 1967–1968. I had met him at the NCO club, and he asked me where I was going. I told him I was assigned to Ubon Royal Thai Air Force Base in Thailand for duty with the Sixteenth Special Operations Squadron.

He looked at me like I was crazy and said, "Those birds are sitting ducks! One was just shot down this year!"

I told him it was what I wanted, and he told me to contact him when I finished snake school (jungle survival). He would arrange a direct flight to Ubon from Clark since they had a daily scatback (T-37) flight going. He said I could take a friend with me if I wished. If I took the regular "klong" flight (a C-130 trash hauler), I would have to stay in Bangkok for a few days. The upcountry shuttle would take all day.

I told him I would let him know, and we went to town. During our training, I made two friends that I especially got along with. Jerry Olson (Oley) was a staff sergeant who was a motorcycle nut. The other was Dwight, a young airman who was just starting out in the air force. I got along with the rest of the people okay, but Oley, Dwight, and I hung out together.

The senior student was kind of a dunderhead, and I didn't get along with him at all. The day finally came when we were set to leave. We were scheduled for the klong in two days. I contacted my buddy and told him I was ready to go. I asked Oley and Dwight if they wanted to come along, but they wanted to spend a couple of days in Bangkok.

I made my arrangements with the first sergeant and was scheduled to leave the next day. I told Oley to tell the student leader when he called my name for roll call to say, "I heard that Dave went AWOL with a Filipino broad." The next morning at 0730, I got on the scatback and hauled ass!

CHAPTER ONE

The Squadron

After three hours, we arrived in Ubon Air Base. The scatback had radioed ahead and told the tower to tell the Sixteenth that they had an incoming crewmember. As I went into the small terminal I was greeted by a tall, sharp-looking technical sergeant with a marine haircut. He looked like a marine NCO. He introduced himself as Technical Sergeant Jack (his call sign was Gunner Jack) and put me in the back of a jeep.

We arrived at the squadron; the first thing I noticed when I entered the building was the emblem right above the entrance door. It was a ghost coming out of a full moon with a blue hood and two 20mm guns blazing. To the right of the front door, a sign said, *Spectre: The Fabulous Four Engine Fighter!* I saw Spectre on all the office doors.

I was introduced around. Everyone from officer to enlisted was very friendly and did their best to make me feel at home. I met the first sergeant, and he indoctrinated me into the squadron. He told me about the outfit's history, its nightly missions, and its outstanding, all-for-one-and-one-for-all mentality. The squadron's theme song was "Ghost Riders in the Sky." It did seem most appropriate.

The Sixteenth SOS call sign Spectre flew modified C-130 aircraft which became the AC-130. The aircraft were painted black and had four turboprop engines. For armament, they had four 20mm guns and four mini guns in portals on the left side of the aircraft. This was the most deadly gunship in the world!

When in the attack mode, the aircraft flew in a 30-degree left bank and circled the target. It went round and round the target so it was not hard for the communist (Gomer) gunners to figure out our position. The

1

pilot varied his altitude and circle width to throw them off, but things got dicey after a few orbits! They flew secret missions into Laos, North Vietnam, South Vietnam, up by the Chinese border, Cambodia, and all over Southeast Asia, interdicting the Ho Chi Minh Trail. The squadron had six aircraft assigned with a normal eleven- or twelve-man crew. There was the pilot, aircraft commander (AC), copilot, flight engineer (FE), table navigator, night-observation device operator, the right scanner, a forward gunner, an aft gunner, two sensor operators, an illuminator operator (IO), and a combat camera man. Each man had a specific job and they all depended on each other for their very survival!

The first sergeant did not mince any words. He said they had lost a gunship that was trying to land at Ubon after being hit by anti-aircraft fire. Everyone bailed out but the pilot, copilot, flight engineer, and IO. The FE and the IO were killed when the plane crashed. The aircraft flew at a maximum of 5,000 feet and was a sitting duck! It depended on the night and the skill of the crew to survive. Most nights, at least one aircraft was hit by anti-aircraft artillery (AAA).

When he asked if I still wanted to spend a year here, I said, "Of course! Where did the name of that fabulous four-engine fighter came from?"

He told me that in early 1969, a Spectre gunship was on an armed recon mission in north Laos. They spotted what appeared to be a communist helicopter flying from North Vietnam into Laos with no lights. They received permission to fire on it and shot it down!

He said, "Then we were off to see the commander and the rest of the crews. The squadron commander was a major. He seemed to be a very professional, friendly man who always looked after his troops. During the dry season (October to April), we will be flying every night full bore. During the wet season, we will still be flying, but the Ho Chi Minh Trail will be flooded out. We will be looking for targets of opportunity!"

There were seven engineers, six IOs, and twenty-something gunners. The majority of them were scheduled to leave as soon as their replacements arrived, including a small number of officers. I was taken to the barracks, which was a Quonset hut. It was called the Bat Cave because it was windowless and had air-conditioning! We were double-bunked, and each enlisted man had one locker. When they were not flying, they were sleeping or at the NCO or airmans club. At the front of the barracks, off-duty men gathered in a small room with two tables and a refrigerator.

I dumped my stuff on a bottom bunk and reported back to the squadron. The "first sergeant" had a clerk take me around the base to check in. Everything went smoothly, but when I got to the dispensary, the flight surgeon told me to take off my shoes; he took my footprints. When I asked why, he said, "These are to identify you if we recover anything when you get shot down! The combats boots are the last thing to burn!"

That got my attention—especially when he said "when." After checking in, most of the squadron was up and ready to fly. The missions started at about 1800. An aircraft would fly for about four and a half hours, return to base, and then a new crew would take it up again. This went on every night—seven days a week! Our last flight would land at about 0600 or right before daylight. It took about thirty-five minutes to get to the trail.

We flew into central Laos or farther, depending upon where we were assigned. When we flew way up north, we had to land at a Thai base to refuel in order to get back to Ubon. When I walked into the gunner section, Sergeant Jackson asked if I was ready to fly.

I answered in the affirmative, and he scheduled me for the next night.

CHAPTER TWO

First Flight

I was assigned to a gun crew, and we reported to the aircraft at 1500 for preflight. I was fascinated with the aircraft and fell in love with it right off the bat. It was huge! It was black, and the Spectre emblem was painted on the left side near the upper fuselage. Inside the aircraft, it was cramped. The booth where the sensor operators sat was in the center on the right. There was a small aisle where the flight crew and gunners could go back and forth.

By the forward crew entrance, there were big binoculars where the night-observation device officer sat on a bicycle seat. There were ammo cans tied down everywhere with extra ammo for the 20mm guns and the mini guns. The lead gunner had me preflight the twenties and arm them to see if I remembered anything from Lockbourne. I passed the test.

After preflight, we went back to the squadron for briefing. We had all our combat gear, and it was the first time I had so much gear on. The aircraft commander briefed the crew on our mission. We were headed for what they called the Iron Triangle. It was called that because there were a whole passel of guns just waiting there! He briefed us on the mission, the bailout route, and our emergency identification signal of the day. I do have to admit that I was a "little" worried when listening to the briefing. He said that if we were hit badly, he would ring the bailout bell—and we better be gone! If any crewmember thought we were out of control and wanted to leave the plane, feel free to do so as a last resort!

He went over the escape and evasion part. I had paid attention in Clark and Washington, but this was for real! I was going into harm's way where a bunch of Gomers were getting ready to shoot me down! The rest of the crew was very calm—just another day at the office!

We got into the crew bus, which was nicknamed "Gertie," and the driver drove us to the flight line. We arrived at a big, black, beautiful monster that looked like it was raring to go into combat. I had mixed feelings about whether I would be up to the task. Everyone was relaxed; they had been doing the same thing for months. I followed along and paid attention to what everyone said.

After the preflight checklist was completed, the pilot started all four engines. Hearing all four of those turboprops sing, I thought, *God help me. I have found a home!*

We taxied out to the runway and took off over the city of Ubon. It was a small city with single-story houses everywhere except for two ten-story buildings. I found out later the two taller buildings were the Ubon Hotel. After circling the city and bore-sighting the computer, we were off to combat. When we crossed the Mekong River (the Fence), the crewmembers suited up in combat gear. For the officers, it included a backpack parachute, but the gunners only had chest packs that we had to put on if we were going to jump. We had survival vests, two radios, four flares, .38 ammo, a KA-BAR knife, and other evasion equipment. We each had two water bottles, a ballistic helmet, and a parachute harness. Some of the gunners wore their .38 pistol on their hips, and others had it on their vests.

After a while, the navigator told the pilot that we were twenty-five miles inside the Fence. We went black in the rear; there were no white lights of any kind. Any lights needed to have red lenses. We armed all the guns and got ready for combat. As we entered the combat area, our pilot reported to the Airborne Command and Control Center (ABCCC) for central Laos. Its call sign was Moonbeam. Its job was to keep track of us and vector us onto any targets they had. They were responsible for the whole area and were very busy.

I was assigned to help any gunner who needed it. When the action started, the instructor gunner wanted me up at the right scanner's window. He was on the right side of the aircraft—right next to number-three engine. We all had headsets so the gunners could talk to each other in private. There was a network just for us so we would not bother the other crewmembers with our chatter. Everyone monitored the main network because the pilot used it.

The AC and the sensors started looking for trucks. We flew up and down the jungle roads with the IR (infrared) sensor and the BC (Black Crow) sensors looking for the heat of the engine and the ignition from the spark plugs.

The IO in the rear yelled, "Triple A, five o'clock, no sweat!"

I looked back and saw a bunch of red balls passing by the aircraft. And all of a sudden they exploded! I thought they were close, but the crew did not seem to be concerned! I damn near had a heart attack!

The IR sensor told the pilot that he had numerous movers (trucks) on and off the road. We prepared to attack! The instructor gunner called me up to the right scanner's window. He told me to look over his shoulder and keep my mouth shut! The pilot put the aircraft in a 30-degree left bank and prepared to fire on the lead truck.

The right scanner called out, "Triple A is accurate! Break right!"

The pilot immediately broke right. I saw seven big red balls go right over the right wing and detonate about two hundred yards away! The right scanner told me they were 37mm shells!

I thought, *God, these Gomers are trying to kill me! And there is nothing I can do about it except shoot back!*

The pilot rolled in and hit the first truck. It exploded in a big ball of fire that really pissed off the gunners on the ground. Three gun sights came up, and they all tried to zero in on the gunship. The pilot flew through the flak and kept up his attack! He hit the next two trucks, and they all exploded, lighting up the ground and sky!

When the pilot was not attacking, he was jinking all over the sky to get away from the enemy fire. We were bounced all over the aircraft, but the gunners and the IO kept at their stations as if it was a normal day at the office! The pilot finally pulled off target and asked the crew to check for battle damage. The enemy rounds were so close that I could hear their hot sizzling sounds as they passed by. I could also smell the cordite! All during this time, I was looking over the right scanner's shoulder. Although I didn't know it, I had hold of his shoulder. He finally told me to let go! I had an iron grip on him; it was as if nothing could happen to me as long as I hung on! We pulled a couple of miles off target, checked our ammo and the aircraft, and then we went back! The sensor spotted more trucks, and the AC didn't waste any time in attacking again! This felt like an eternity, but it actually was about four hours!

When we finally ran out of ammunition (Winchester), the AC called for RTB (return to base). As we crossed the Mekong back into Thailand, we cleaned up the aircraft, picking up all the spent brass and putting it in big canvas bags. We always brought back our spent brass.

We finally went white in the rear. Lights went on, and the gunners razzed my ass! I looked like I had just gotten out of the shower! I had to admit that it was a rush like no other! I had found out that I had the guts to fly in combat in a kill-or-be-killed situation! We finally landed at Ubon and were met by Gertie. The officers went off to intel, and we went into Spectre ops. We put away our combat gear and went to the NCO club.

I felt as if I had been born again! I really loved flying combat! And the people I flew with were the greatest! They were all so calm and professional—even when looking death in the face. I could not think of any other place I would rather be! We all sat at one table and ordered ten beers at once! I was charged to buy the first round since I was the new guy! Since beer was only ten cents a can, I bought the first five rounds! After that rush of combat, it didn't take too much to get us feeling good.

Hank's band played "Ghost Riders" a few times! I was home!

CHAPTER THREE

Oley Arrives

Two days later, Oley and the rest of the new guys arrived. They were taken to Spectre operations. Oley told me the first thing that the student leader said to the first shirt was that he had one man AWOL! He told Homer (the first shirt's name) that technical Sergeant Burns had gone AWOL in the PI over a woman. Homer looked at him and asked if he was talking about Technical Sergeant Dave Burns.

Stupid said yes! Homer told him that not only was I not AWOL, but I had already flown two combat missions! Stupid looked dumfounded and then looked at Oley like he wanted to kill him! Oley had an innocent look on his face!

When the on-duty NCO brought the new guys to the barracks, I saw Oley. I was drinking a Coke when they walked in. Stupid didn't say a word to me; he just walked in the back and got a bunk. I already had one reserved for Oley. As soon as he put his gear on it, we went to the club. He filled me in on his mission in Bangkok. We talked for about an hour, and then I told him I had to get ready for another mission. When I reported to the gunner section, I asked Jack if I could have Oley on my crew when I got qualified. He said yes.

Oley and the rest of the new guys finished checking in and drawing their combat gear. It would be another three days before they got their first mission. In that period, I was almost qualified to be a full-fledged gunner. Because of my rank, I was going to be a gun crew chief. I had to have ten combat missions to qualify to wear my combat aircrew wings on a permanent basis.

As soon as Oley was through checking in, we went downtown to the Okay Hat Shop to get our Spectre hats. The hat shop was the only one in Ubon that could do the job. The black hats had "Spectre" embroidered in the front, aircrew wings in the middle, and "AC-130 Gunship" under the wings. I bought three of them, and Oley bought two.

I took two of my K2B flight suits down there to be dyed black. At that time, I was the only one in the squadron with a black flight suit. No one gave me any grief; before long, most of the gunners had black suits. We could fly in our combat fatigues, our K2B, or the black flight suit.

Oley and I walked around Ubon. I said, "God help me, Oley, but I love this place!"

The people were so friendly, and flying combat was what I had always wanted to do. He just looked at me like I was on something!

CHAPTER FOUR

The Men of Spectre

From December 1969 until March 1970, we were very short on personnel. We did not have enough pilots, navs, or sensor operators to go around. In addition, we only had six flight engineers, seven IOs, and twenty-something gunners. The original crew was completing their year; as soon as one of us was qualified, one of them left. So we were flying every night.

We would fly ten nights straight, work loading crew one night, and then get a night off. When we were not flying, we were in the club or downtown getting acquainted with the "locals." There was a resentment of the enlisted crewmembers from the ground-pounders because we were considered the "elite" of the air force. The non-flyers were working twelve-hour days, six days a week, paying income taxes, and not getting any of the benefits we were getting. We were drawing tax-exempt flight pay and combat pay. We were also getting paid to eat off base since our flight hours precluded us from eating in the base chow hall! And we lived in an air-conditioned hut!

We always traveled in groups of three or more. Wherever we went, we stuck together like glue, and the base personnel were always looking at us with distaste. We ate most of our meals at the NCO club or the airman's club. We would take up three tables at a time; this did not sit well with the ground-pounders. The Thai waitresses would serve us first because we tipped them every time they served us. The biggest reason they did not like us was because they had been ordered to Ubon, and it showed in their attitudes. We were all volunteers and wanted to be here. When we got back from a combat mission, we let it all hang out! It was so good to be alive!

There were fights or arguments with the ground-pounders most every night. In the clubs, they would get drunk and yell, "Spectre sucks!"

We would usually respond with a left hook! The officers had it a little better. Most of the officers at Ubon were fighter jocks, and some flew escort for us on occasion. Although all of the officers and enlisted men of the squadron were outstanding, there were a few who really stood out. The squadron commander, Major Hight, was an outstanding officer who always looked out for his men.

There were many officers who were great! I had never been in the company of such outstanding, brave officers! The flight engineers were older than the gunners. They were all volunteers—and were motivated and dedicated to their jobs. The illuminator operators and the gunners were mostly young hard-chargers who really enjoyed their jobs! A few were considered over the hill at thirty-plus, but most of them were teeny boppers who were just made for their jobs!

In the regular air force, they would have probably gotten in trouble for their independent thinking. In Spectre, they were expected and encouraged to think for themselves and do their duties—no matter what. Most of them did just that!

One of the gunners I knew for a long while was named Joe. His call sign was "Spectre Joe." When I got to the squadron, he was on leave. When he returned, we became good friends. An engineer named Bob could play a mean fiddle. When we were not flying, we were hanging around in the hooch. He would break out his fiddle. He had quite a stack of country music, and something was always on his tape recorder. His favorite was "Sunday Morning Coming Down" by Lynn Anderson.

I met the biggest black IO in the world. Arthur Humphrey had been in the squadron for a few months, and he was already a legend! He was a technical sergeant, was six foot five and 220 pounds. He was the coolest person in the aircraft when we were under attack. From the ramp in the back of the aircraft, he hung out and dropped flares when the pilot needed them. The flare-launcher on the right aft side of the aircraft contained twenty-four parachute flares. Arthur also called out anti-aircraft fire that was directed at the aircraft. He always hung out farther than the other IOs. He was attached to the aircraft by a cable attached to the top of the plane. The other end was attached to his parachute harness.

On one mission, he yelled, "Accurate Triple A break right!"

The pilot broke violently right to escape the rounds! After the pilot rolled out, Arthur called and asked him for permission to come aboard! During the breakaway, Arthur had fallen out of the aircraft and was hanging by his cable! The pilot told him to get his big ass back in the aircraft and to quit playing around!

I flew with him on my fifth mission. I was training to be the right scanner; when he called out accurate fire, it sure was accurate! I could hear the rounds sizzle as they went by the aircraft. We were flying so low—between 4,000 and 5,000 feet—that we worried about direct hits and near misses. We were hit twice on that mission, but it was mostly shrapnel hitting the fuselage and the wing. I could smell the cordite when the rounds went off. The pilot would pull off target and check the damage. We would attack again if it was not too bad.

As soon as we landed, the maintenance crews would patch up the holes—and off we would go again. After ten combat missions, a gunner was entitled to wear his combat wings for the rest of his air force career—no matter where he was assigned. On my tenth mission, I was with Oley and Dwight. There was a full moon, and the instructor gunner put me in the right scanner's seat! We were fragged to the Iron Triangle and picked up more than five hundred rounds of AAA in three hours! We had four near misses and destroyed fifteen trucks!

I was becoming addicted to flying. When I was not scheduled, I volunteered to fly for anyone who did not want to fly for one reason or another! I looked forward to getting over the jungle, shooting, and being shot at. I loved the thrill of dodging anti-aircraft fire! In short, I was kind of nuts!

Every week, new guys would be assigned to the squadron from the States. They were hard to come by since it was a volunteer mission. In the air force, there was a shortage of people who volunteered to get shot at nightly! The men we did get were the cream of the crop! Most of them were young airmen and buck sergeants. There were a few staff sergeants and tech sergeants. There were not many tech and above. The Palace Gun recruiter at Randolph Air Force Base, Technical Sergeant Brian Morrison, sent only the best to us.

After about two weeks, Oley moved downtown with a Teelock (Thai lady). When we finished flying, we would hang around the club for a while until he went "home." The missions continued every night, and the battle damage seemed to get worse! One aircraft had a 37mm go off in the wheel well, and it punched holes all over the plane. No one was wounded, but the plane was down for a week. That left just five available for nightly missions. The new guys were just the kind of people we needed. There was Technical Sergeant Ron "Sweet Gin" Branson, Staff Sergeant Kevin Mullaney, and Sergeant Don B.

Around my fifteenth mission, I decided I was going to be the first of the new guys to fly a hundred missions! I set out to do just that. Whenever I had a day off, I would ask if anyone wanted me to fly for them. I never got turned down. The only restriction was we could only fly once per day. Since it ended at midnight, I could land at 2300 and take off again at 0100!

CHAPTER FIVE

Ubon Nightlife

In Ubon, there was a street with five bars on it. They were named the Fairlane, the Jaguar, the See Saw, the Corsair, and another smaller bar. They all had bands and women galore! There were bars right outside the gates. Across the street were the Old Playboy (Sampan) Club and the New Playboy.

There was no shortage of places where you could go to "relax!" And the men of Spectre did just that! We were all known in town, and most places welcomed us! It could be that we all had money—and were willing to spend it. All the bands knew how to play "Ghost Riders" and did so whenever we were in the place. Of course, a hundred-baht tip was always appreciated.

We always went downtown in a group and stayed together until the women showed up. Then we would E&E (escape and evade) to the lady's house. When we weren't flying and being shot at, we were downtown enjoying life. But that was not very often at first. The bars closed at midnight; all the ladies who did not have any customers—and the men who were still looking—would go to the Ubon Hotel. On the ninth floor, there was a big restaurant/bar with a band. We called it "the pigpen in the sky"! It was crowded for the first two weeks after payday.

All the ladies who worked the bars were required to have a "VD card." It had their photos on it; they were checked by doctors every week to make sure they were clean! One gunner sat by the elevator when he was downtown, and he would check the ladies' VD cards. He always chose the one with the most recent date! It didn't do him to much good as he had to visit the doctor twice during his tour! I went to the doctor and got myself one of those VD cards. I had my photo put on it and showed it to the ladies! They thought that was cool and asked me how I got one of them! Every week, I would have a gunner sign me off on the card!

Since I was married and had two kids, I would send most of my money home. However, I had thirty-two envelopes, and I gave myself five dollars a day to live on. Whatever I had left over at the end of the day, I would put in the thirty-second envelope and consider that my "party" envelope. It grew into a good amount with beer ten costing cents a can and grease burgers costing twenty-five cents apiece!

Every chance we got, Oley and I would go downtown. It didn't take long for him to pick up a permanent Teelock!

CHAPTER SIX

Dry Season

From January on, it was all-out flying on the trail. There were hundreds of trucks going to South Vietnam on the Ho Chi Minh Trail. Every night we went out to intercept and destroy as many as we could. Of course, it was not a cakewalk; there were aircraft being hit every night. Luckily, most of the hits were shrapnel, but a few put big holes in the wings and fuselage. We got word that the air force was going to increase the number of aircraft and try to get more volunteers to join up, but we were still short in 1970.

On my way to a hundred missions, I flew twenty-one days in February. I was hit twice and received over 8,000 rounds of Triple A! On 9 February, we flew into the Iron Triangle and destroyed eight trucks and set off thirty-seven secondary explosions! We hit an ammo dump. The gunners on the ground went crazy and tried really hard to shoot us down. March was outstanding! I flew twenty-six days, destroyed fifty-six trucks—and one snake on the runway! I lost count of the Triple A, but it was way up there.

Gunner Gene Fields was from West Virginia. He was about five foot five and didn't weigh very much. His call sign was "Short Round." The boy was always getting into something. One day when I woke up in the afternoon, I was shaving in the bathroom. The air police brought him in; he was drunker than a skunk! They asked me if Gene belonged to us. I told them I would take care of him. I picked him up and was taking him to the Bat Cave. He pulled the toothbrush out of my mouth and started to brush my hair! The boy was wasted! I put him to bed; since he had the day off, I let him sleep it off. He was a good kid, but when he wasn't flying, he let it all hang out—as most of us did.

CHAPTER SEVEN

The Warlord

April started out with a bang. The flying weather was good. The Gomer gunners were getting better every day, but we still had a job to do. On 5 April, we went into the Iron Triangle again. We got eighteen trucks, but we picked up 685 rounds of Triple A and six rockets! That was one of the few times they fired rockets at us.

On 9 April, we went back there with Major Wilson and Arthur Humphrey. We picked up 1,022 rounds of Triple A and two rockets! That was the most rounds that had been fired at me. The AC spent most of his time dodging the anti-aircraft fire, and Arthur was constantly calling out "Break right!" or "Break left!"

I was in the scanner window, and it was just as bad there. A few times, we didn't know which way to break—so we just sucked it up! The whole damn sky smelled like cordite! We spent four hours on target and then came back home. The trip back to base was a time for reflection for everyone on the aircraft. It was really quiet for a while on the intercom, and then the AC asked if we wanted to go back! We told him we didn't have enough ammo or toilet paper aboard!

On 21 April, we went to the November area on a recon mission. We saw many trucks there, and we rolled in to attack the trucks. The full moon was so bright the gunners on the ground could see us for part of our orbit. It was so bad that we just could not get a clear shot off. We stayed for three hours and then came back to base.

Our aircraft was nicknamed "The Warlord." When we landed, the maintenance chief asked if the plane was operational. The pilot said it was. We reloaded it for another crew and went into the personal equipment room to put up our gear. Gene and his crew were there; they had been scheduled to take off at 2300, but their aircraft was broken. We had landed at midnight, and they were scheduled to take our plane.

The aircraft commander (Major Brooks) and most of his crew had been through gunship school with me, and I knew them well. His nickname was "Brass Balls Billy" because he was fearless and could hang in there. I asked Gene where he was going.

He said, "To the November area."

I explained how I had just come from there; the area was really hot and had a whole bunch of guns. I told him to watch his ass since the full moon was bright enough to see the ground and the river.

After Gene and his crew took off, we went to the club to unwind. Another flight crew had landed; we were all listening to Hank's band and scarfing beers. At about 0200, the club manager took to the bandstand and announced that all Spectre flight crews were to report to Spectre operations at once—by order of the squadron commander!

We were half-ripped, but orders were orders. When we arrived at operations, all the guys were looking really grim. The commander got all of us in the briefing room and told us that *625* had been shot down! He did not have any information on any survivors, but all of us were restricted to the Bat Cave. The officers were restricted to their rooms until further orders!

We were in shock; all of us had been told that something like this was bound to happen sooner or later, but we never really thought it would happen. Our planes had been shot up numerous times, but they had always been able to make it back to base. We waited for further information about how many had survived. There were eleven men on the crew; I hoped that all of them had gotten out of the aircraft.

Each man was lost in his own thoughts. The area they were shot down in was heavy with North Vietnamese soldiers and Laotian Gomers. Anyone who had ever been shot down in Laos and was captured had never been seen again.

The night passed very slowly, and we still had not gotten any word about any survivors. The only information we got was that the Fortieth Air Rescue Squadron in Udorn was in the area and looking for survivors. Those guys had giant balls; we knew that any of them who made it out would get back if the Gomers did not get them first.

At about 0500, the commander got us together again. The only information he had was that the aircraft had been hit in the tail section.

There had only been one Mayday. An F-4 in the area saw the fire on the ground; as he was leaving the area, he had heard one beeper! Only one! Each crewmember had two survival radios on him; if he hit the ground alive, he was to activate one of his radios in beeper mode to let anyone in the area know he was alive. When the rescue people honed in on the beeper, he would make voice contact to let the aircraft know if he was injured or not. The aircraft would call in other fighters to protect his area until the Jolly Greens air rescue helicopter arrived and plucked him out of the jungle!

After three hours, there was still only one beeper activated. After voice contact, he was identified as Gene Fields, the gunner. Only one out of eleven! Gene was burned, but the Jollies had picked him up and taken him to the hospital in Danang, South Vietnam.

There was no further word, but the commander told us that, as soon as he knew something, we would also know. We were informed that the missions were still on and nothing had changed. When the restriction to the barracks was lifted, the commander told us to get some rest and food and to play it cool with the rest of the base.

One out eleven was quite a shocker; we did not know the whole story. It would be a year until we got the word from Gene. From Danang, he was taken to Japan and then transferred to the burn center in Texas. All we really knew was that he was alive.

The mood of the squadron changed overnight from individuals flying and personal problems to one of determination to get payback. We grew even closer—officer and enlisted. When we went to the club, we were surrounded with well-wishers. There were many questions—but none that we could answer.

I was scheduled with Major Dyer to fly the first mission at sunset. My crew and I went to the flight line, checked our aircraft, preflighted the guns, and then went to operations to await the nightly briefing. When we were all assembled, the squadron commander came in and told us we were going into the same area where *625* had been shot down. We were to do two things: constantly check for beepers and look for trucks. We were told to be extra careful to watch out for the guns since it was a 37mm AA gun that had gotten *625*.

We were to have an F-4 escort from the 497 TFS in Ubon. He was to suppress any gun activity if possible. He left, and Major Dyer told us that he was going after that goddamn gun—and he was going to get it! And if anyone was unwilling to go along, now was the time to say so. None of us objected.

We took off on time, armed all the guns—the minis and the twenties. We were all primed for action; to say that the butterflies weren't there is a misstatement. But our rage was more powerful, and our senses were primed. The sun had set when we got on target; we immediately went into attack mode. All our radios were tuned into the rescue channels, and we were looking for any and all trucks. After about thirty minutes, a gun came up at us from our eleven o'clock position. It was the same location of the gun that had gotten *625*.

Arthur said, "No sweat."

We continued in orbit. After our third orbit, two guns came up. One was accurate.

I yelled, "Break left!"

The aircraft commander told the nod to place his sight on the gun. We went around again, and the AC told the F-4 above to get ready. We were going to challenge the gun! There is no feeling on earth that compares to getting into a gunfight with a determined enemy! As soon as we came up, the 37mm guns came up full blast!

Major Dyer asked for all eight guns, and we let them have it! We both used tracers, and it was like the Fourth of July. Our guns hit right in the gun pit, but he kept firing! The F-4 dove in and unloaded two napalm bombs right on the pit! Direct hit! Nothing but teeth, hair, and eyeballs were all over the place! We kept firing into the second pit; the F-4 made another dive and dropped two 750-pound bombs.

Everything went quiet after that. We continued in orbit, hoping for more guns to come up, but they were not about to go through that again. Major Dyer had completely expended our ammo on those two guns: 6,000 rounds of 20mm ammo and 10,000 rounds of mini gun ammo. The barrels were hot and probably warped. We told the F-4 to expend all his remaining ordnance on the gun pit fires, and he dropped two more napalm bombs in the area. He ignited a secondary explosion; we figured he had gotten the ammo dump for the guns. We RTB'd, and we let go of our emotions as soon as we crossed the Fence. We were certain we had gotten the gun that had shot down *625* and another one for good measure. It felt like a heavy weight had been lifted off our shoulders. We were back in the fight—stronger and more together then ever!

We went to the club, but there was no one there from Spectre. The crews started showing up after they landed. Two other crews had gone into the area for a beeper check, and they had seen the fires we lit. They had not been shot at. It was a small victory.

After three days of searching, the crew was declared MIA. We had a memorial service for them in the base chapel, and all the enlisted flight crews marched in formation to the chapel for the services.

The Story of *625*

This was told to me about a year later by a friend of Gene Fields, who had heard about it firsthand. They had been in their third orbit when they were hit in the tail section. The round hit the flare launcher on the right aft side of the plane. It ignited the flares, and an extremely hot fire broke out. Gene was working the aft 20mm guns; the flames drove him forward. The IO on the ramp could not get free of his safety cable and was killed by the flames. The AC told everyone to remain calm; at the time, he did not know about the fire. The officers in the booth were unable to get out because of the heat, and they were also killed outright.

The pilot had control of the airplane and was keeping it straight to give everyone a chance to bail out. Gene was about to be overcome with the heat and smoke and was burnt on his face and hands. He had his chute on, and the flames drove him forward. He went out of the right scanner's window. He did not see any of the gunners or the right scanner when he went out. He assumed they were already gone or overcome by the toxic smoke and flames.

As his chute opened, he saw the plane descending in flames on a controlled-level flight path and impacting the ground. Major Brooks had control of the plane until the very end. It took a lot of guts to remain with the aircraft until the end. It must have been horrible, but the flight engineer, navigator, and copilot remained at their stations until the very end.

The Crew

Major William Brooks, aircraft commander
First Lieutenant John Towle, copilot
Lieutenant Colonel Charles Rowley, table navigator

Lieutenant Colonel Charles Davis, night-observation device officer
Major Don Fisher, infrared operator
Master Sergeant Robert Ireland, flight engineer
Sergeant Ronnie Hensley, illuminator operator
Sergeant Thomas Adachi, aerial gunner
Sergeant Stephen Harris, aerial gunner
Airman First Class Donald Lint, aerial gunner

I had attended gunship and survival schools with six of those men. It was heartbreaking when the casualty assistance officers came to the Bat Cave and cleaned out the crew's lockers to send their personal stuff home!

The nightly missions continued with a fever pitch. We had been bloodied—but not defeated! We were aware that this could and would happen again, but not a man quit flying. If anything, they became more determined than ever to wreak havoc on the Ho Chi Minh Trail.

The aircraft kept coming back with holes, but the nightly truck kills were improving dramatically. I kept up my pursuit to reach a hundred missions as soon as possible. In April, I flew a total of twenty-five missions.

On 28 April, we flew with Major Ken Wilson. Call sign "Old Gray Fox" was one of the best pilots we had—and we had a bunch. Arthur was the IO, and we were fragged to the Juliette area. The trucks were running hot and heavy; we destroyed twelve and received 1,380 rounds of Triple A fire—in four hours! There were many near misses and a couple of holes in the fuselage from shrapnel. The Fox was playing the airplane like an organ; he would bob, weave, change altitude, and speed while firing on the trucks! It was quite a ride; after it was over, we thought we had been in a steam bath! After we landed, we went to the club and had a few dozen beers to unwind.

At about nine in the morning, the squadron clerk came to the Bat Cave. He got Arthur and me out of bed and told us that the commander wanted to see us. Arthur and I were probably the two biggest men in the squadron. When we got to the squadron, the commander told us to go to the officer's hooch area. We were to bring a captain down to the squadron—by force, if necessary!

We looked at him and asked, "Just how much force should we use?"

He said, "Just get him here—and don't accept any excuses!"

We took his jeep and went looking for this "captain." We knocked on his hooch door, but he did not answer. We knocked again, told him who we were, and said that the squadron commander wanted to see him at once.

He told us to get lost. He wasn't going anywhere with us.

We pushed the door in, got him on his feet, and told him to get dressed. He was coming with us—buck naked or dressed properly. He looked at us and thought about it for about twenty seconds before he put on his flight suit and came with us with no trouble.

After we delivered him to the commander, we were excused. We asked the first shirt what was up. He told us that he would explain later. Since we were up, we went to the club for breakfast. About forty-five minutes later, the first shirt saw us in the club. He told us the captain had refused to fly a combat mission and walked out of the briefing room, leaving his crew without a pilot. He went to his room and refused to come out for any reason—that's why the commander had sent us to get him. The commander chewed his ass good, had him pack his gear, and got him off the base at once. He was sent to Saigon with a recommendation for discharge due to cowardice! He was the only officer who ever quit! The story got around that Arthur and I were the mafia for the commander.

May started off with a bang. We were flying *628* with Bennie the Bean. Lieutenant Colonel Bennie Castillo was another hard-charger; he used to wear a big sombrero out to the aircraft. Every chance we got, we would try to steal it—but no luck! In four and a half hours, we destroyed ten trucks and received over 300 rounds of Triple A fire. They didn't hit us, but they scared the hell out of us!

CHAPTER EIGHT

My 100

I flew nineteen days in May. On 24 May, (my 99th mission) my crew flew with Hoppy the Pilot (Major Riopel), one of the most outstanding pilots. We went to the Barrel Roll area near the Chinese border and North Vietnam. It was another full moon, and Arthur was the IO. Oley was in the scanner's window, and I was working the aft twenties.

We were flying AC-628 through mountains and unchartered terrain. When we were 5,000 feet above the roads—about 9,000 feet altitude—we discovered three tanks! We rolled in with the twenties, but they were ineffective. They just bounced off the turrets! Then all hell broke loose! We received over 2,560 rounds of most every kind of Triple A. There were 37mm, 57mm, and 23mm SZU quad guns.

Hoppy stayed with the targets and called for fast movers with hard bombs to get the tanks. We played tag with the guns; after about thirty minutes, we got two F-4s from Udorn Air Base. We sparkled for the fighters (fired tracers at the tanks) to give the fighters a location. They rolled in and got all three!

We hauled ass for home, but we did not have enough fuel. We had to land at Udorn to refuel. On 25 May, I flew my hundredth mission on *490* into the November area. Major Overman was my AC. He was another outstanding pilot. His call sign was "Tonto" because he was part Indian.

It was a typical night; we received 331 rounds of Triple A. When we landed, I bought the rounds and stayed in the NCO club for about three hours. The club operated on a twenty-four-hour basis and was always open when we landed. I was finally authorized to wear a hundred-mission patch on my party suit. I also wore it on my flight suit.

CHAPTER NINE

Tchepone

Tchepone was the one place in Laos that we did not want to fly into. The village was at a crossroads of four highways leading in from Vietnam, the Mugia Pass, the Ban Kari Pass, and the Barthelme Pass. The highways then headed south to the Ho Chi Minh Trail. It was highly defended with all sorts of anti-aircraft guns. Going there was a guarantee of being hit or being shot down, but we had to go into the area all the time except during the full moon.

I flew there with the Gray Fox, but he could not get off a good shot for the first hour! The guns would wait until we started our orbit, and then they would all come up in a barrage in an attempt to shoot us down. He finally got a couple of shots off and hit two trucks that blew up in a bright ball of fire! There were truck parks in the area where the trucks would wait until sunset to start driving the trail. That is when we would show up to attack them. It was a very dangerous place to be at all times; we would usually return to base with a few holes in the aircraft.

We decided to go down the road a few miles from the village and then attack the trucks when they left the safety of Tchepone. The hunting was really good there; each aircraft would bag at least a dozen trucks. The NVA started to put AAA guns on some of the trucks on the trail. Spectre still attacked without regard to safety. There would be at least one Spectre prowling the Tchepone area nightly.

New crewmembers started to arrive almost on a weekly basis; since they had all attended the gunship and survival schools, we put them in the system right away. They were required to fly ten training missions before they could operate in a crew as a full-fledged member. Most of them were airman first class, but there were a few sergeants and staff sergeants. All of them were motivated by the mission!

Our contact and supervisor at Randolph AFB in Texas was Master Sergeant Brian P. Morrison. He recruited hardheaded, motivated young airmen who did not mind being shot at nightly! He ran the Palace Gun program. This was not normal air force procedure. Normally there were only a few combat units that were actually being shot at—usually the air rescue guys in Danang and Udorn.

In May, I got my call sign on a permanent basis. On 7 May, we were flying up in the barrel roll looking for trucks. We had a new pilot who couldn't hit his targets. He was firing all around the trucks without hitting them. I was kind of salty then; I told him I was going to go into the booth to change into my battle costume.

When I emerged, I called him and said, "Okay, pilot. This is Captain Spectre speaking! I'm taking over the aft guns. Now kill something!"

He was flabbergasted, but he went along with it. Lo and behold, when he fired the aft guns, he got two kills! He said that Captain Spectre was to fly with him from now on and told me to leave Dave Burns home! The name stuck. I went downtown and got my Chinese buddy to make me a black cape with the Spectre emblem on it and the words "Captain Spectre." I wore the cape to all the parties!

There was an excellent Thai restaurant about a block from the main gate. Some of the crewmembers would go there to grab a bite prior to flying. About three weeks after *625* was shot down, I was drinking a beer in the NCO club with my crew when the club master-at-arms came in and said there was a phone call for any Spectre gunner. I answered the phone. A gun crew chief was at the Thai restaurant with his crew, and they were being harassed by four drunken grunts.

They were saying, "It looks like Spectre finally got what's coming to them. It serves them right; I hope it happens again!"

I told him to hang loose and I would be right there. My crew and I "unassed" the NCO club and headed to the restaurant. As we walked in, our demeanor was such that the Thais suspected a problem and started to make way. The drunks saw us come in and damn near fainted! I walked up to the gun crew chief and asked him where the loudmouth was. He said all of them were bad-mouthing Spectre. I told him to enjoy his meal and said that we would handle it! One of the drunks got up in an attempt to apologize. I told him it was too late for that; to badmouth Spectre was one thing, but to badmouth the dead was unforgivable! It was time to pay the piper! I grabbed for him, and he beat feet to the bathroom. The other three scattered like a bunch of rats; one of them even jumped through the open window! Oley put his foot in one guy's ass as he was running away! The whole thing did not last more than a minute. We went back to the club, and the crew went on to fly.

About an hour later, the first shirt came into the NCO club and told us that he had heard something about Dave Burns and crew starting a row in the restaurant. I told him the story, and he told us to forget about it—well done!

The Presidential Unit Citation

During the last week in May 1970, the squadron was notified that we were going to be presented the Presidential Unit Citation for action on the Ho Chi Minh Trail. This was quite an honor as the citation was given to wings and divisions—never to a small squadron. We were told to get into our 1505 uniforms for the presentation by the Seventh Air Force commander.

The squadron did not have enough men assigned to make a formation! We had to borrow some people from other squadrons in the Eighth TAC Fighter Wing! Having to stand at attention while the Sixteenth Special Operations Squadron was presented the award did not sit too well with the enlisted men! There was a lot of bitching in the ranks, but we told them to suck it up! It wasn't every day that they could stand next to greatness! The ceremony did not last too long. He read the citation, congratulated the squadron commander, made a speech and told us how good we were and how proud he was of us. Then he hauled ass back to Saigon.

The citation read as such:

By Virtue of the Authority vested in me as President
of the United States, I have today awarded
the Presidential Unit Citation (Air Force)
for Extraordinary Heroism
to the
Sixteenth Special Operations Squadron
United States Air Force

The Sixteenth Special Operations Squadron, Pacific Air Forces, distinguished itself by extraordinary heroism in connection with military operations against an opposing armed force in Southeast Asia, from 1 December 1969 to 1 March 1970. During this period members of the Sixteenth Special Operations Squadron flew more than 580 combat sorties, resulting in the destruction of more than 1,300 trucks, damage to over 560 other trucks, and over 3,000 secondary fires and explosions. Despite intensive hostile air defenses, uncharted mountainous terrain, and inclement weather, the crewmembers of this squadron nightly risked their lives to deny the enemy free movement of his men and material. By the destruction of vital supplies and munitions destined for enemy troops. The squadron was instrumental in furthering Allied goals in Southeast Asia. The professionalism, dedication to duty, and extraordinary heroism demonstrated by members of the Sixteenth Special Operations Squadron are in keeping with the finest traditions of the military service and reflect the highest credit upon themselves and the Armed Forces of the United States.

Signed
Richard M. Nixon

After the presentation, we all went to the NCO club, and Hank's band played a round of "Ghost Riders." It was a proud day for a small band of airmen—both officers and enlisted. One of the smallest squadrons in the United States Air Force had won one of the highest honors!

The nightly missions continued. We got the training AC-130 in from Ohio, and we were back to six aircraft. We were also slowly getting more crewmembers; rumor had it that the air force was increasing our aircraft because we were causing so much death and destruction on the trail. It would be a while until they got here, and the nightly missions continued.

June was the start of the rainy season. The truck traffic was reduced by the rain and mud. There were nights where we only managed to kill ten or fifteen. The guns were still shooting, and the gunners were getting better each night. Because we had to fly in a left-hand orbit, it did not take long to track us. Things got hairy really fast. Not a night went by without us being thrown around the plane due to jinking and dodging the Triple A! The pilots were getting really good at playing chicken with the gunners; every now and then, the gunners would get lucky and put a hole in us. Luckily, the holes weren't fatal.

One night, Arthur and I flew with Major Riopel up to the barrel roll. We were looking for trucks, and the weather was miserable with thunder, lightning, and rain. We didn't see a thing; we just flew around boring holes in the sky. After three hours, we came back to Ubon. We didn't fire a shot. Arthur and I went to the stag bar in the club to have a few beers before hitting the sack. It was about three o'clock in the morning, and there were only three or four people there. We had a couple dollars between us—enough for about three beers apiece.

A "bug catcher in white" who worked in the dispensary started badmouthing us. He said, "You Spectre guys think you are so hot, but I know you don't do anything!"

Since we were tired, a little wet, and didn't feel like busting heads, I told him a war story. I was getting good at that!

I said, "Boy, where do you think we just came from? We just got back from a hellish combat mission in Hanoi! We took off from Ubon, flew up by the Chinese border, dodged MiGs, flew into North Vietnam, went right to downtown Hanoi on Tudo Street, and shot up the trucks and soldiers." I screwed up; Tudo Street was in Saigon not Hanoi!

Arthur and I finished our beers. He said, "Dave, let's go. I ain't got no more money."

The bug catcher said, "Never mind! I'll pay!"

I told him a hell of a story, but I slipped up when I told him that we had to fly over the Himalayas because of battle damage! But he didn't catch it. At 0430, he was a convert. He worshipped Spectre, and Arthur and I were drunk. We went to the Bat Cave. He got a good war story, and we got free drinks! Everybody made out!

CHAPTER TEN

Sockey Game

About the first week in June, there were a group of us scarfing beers in the Bat Cave.

Major Overman came in and said, "I'm looking for volunteers to take on the visiting Special Forces officers."

We looked at him like he had lost his mind!

He said he needed six men. He made me a major and the others lieutenants and captains. The game was to be played in the officers' club. When we got there, we asked him what "sockey" was and how to play it.

He said it was very simple. "You put ice and water on the floor, put two chairs on each end of the room, take a beer can, bend it in, and try to kick the can between the other team's chairs!"

It sounded simple enough. Ron Broyles was the goalie, and the rest were out on the floor. We asked him what the rules were.

He said, "None!"

The game started with us kicking the can; all of a sudden, I found myself on my back! I had been coldcocked by one of the other officers! It was a knockdown, drag-out game! Our clothes were torn off! There were bruises all over us, but we gave as well as we got! We finally won the game 2-1! Then we all went to the front of the club and got drunk!

The next day, most of us were in the NCO club for breakfast when some of the "officers" from the Special Forces team walked in. They had done just what Tonto had done! They ran their NCO's in to the game, believing that the Spectre officers were "pussies" and didn't stand a chance!

During the missions in June, I had a lot of time to think about *625* being shot down. I kept thinking of those men and the last minutes of their lives. It took unbelievable guts to keep the aircraft in a normal descending flight to give anyone left in the back time to bail out. I tried to envision Major Brooks seeing the ground coming up and knowing that he was going to die. And he still did his duty! No one else got out of the plane except Gene Fields. Those men were brave beyond words—as I would come to find out.

In July, Major Hight was replaced as squadron commander and returned to the States. We had quite a party for him and would miss his leadership a lot. His replacement, Lieutenant Colonel Y. A. Tucker, was another enlisted man's commander. He continued to fight for better berthing for the enlisted flyers. We were double-bunked in the Bat Cave, and it was getting really crowded. He finally got us a bigger barracks, and we had more room for regular lockers.

We started getting the new aircraft in. They were armed with the 40mm guns in the rear (where the two 20mm guns had been before). These guns gave us far more firepower, and we could even go tank-hunting now. They enabled us to get to higher altitudes, which gave us a better chance to dodge the enemy's Triple A.

We got two aircraft in during the rainy season, and there were more on the way. When we were not training, the commander got us out of Ubon on R&R. The base commander was glad to see us leave the base; it kept the friction down. Nine of us went to Clark Field in the Philippines for a seven-day R&R! It was the first time we were able to get away from flying in almost a year. We stayed at the Oasis Hotel, which had an illegal gambling casino—and there were bars galore! Time passed way too fast. We had to go to the flight line to get our plane back to Ubon! We all staggered down to the flight line to board our aircraft. One of the gunners yelled at the crew chief, "We'll give you a hundred dollars to break this plane!"

The crew chief yelled back, "It's broke!"

Major Dyer, the AC, heard this and said, "Like hell it is!"

The crew chief said, "Really, sir. It is broke. It needs a spare part and will take a day to fix!"

When we heard that, we all broke for the terminal and headed back to the Oasis.

About halfway back to the terminal, someone asked, "Where's Joe?"

He had fallen asleep in the plane. We got his ass up and went back to partying! When we got back to Ubon, Colonel Tucker volunteered Arthur

Humphrey and me to go to Udorn Air Base. The Jolly Green Giants were holding a celebration of their hundredth rescue, which turned out to be Gene Fields. They wanted a couple of men from Spectre to attend. We did not know it at the time, but the first shirt volunteered us. A Spectre gunship flew us up there and dropped us off. The aircraft commander, Major Ken Wilson, told Jolly operations that he would be back to pick us up in three days. He added, "And please keep them alive until then."

We were met at the plane by a pararescue man. Technical Sergeant Wayne Fisk had been the PJ who had rescued Gene and pulled him aboard the helicopter. He took us to the Jolly Green barracks, gave us a bunk, and told us that the "party" would start in about an hour!

The men of the Fortieth ARRS had an outstanding reputation for rescuing downed aviators. They would go where other sane men would not even think of going. And their motto, "That others may live," was deserved. They were loved by all flyers because we knew they would spare no effort to rescue us if we were on the ground. To leave us behind was not in their playbook; a lot of Jollies were shot down and killed trying to rescue other downed airmen!

Arthur and I wore our black flight suits all the time we were there. I don't remember getting any sleep for the full three days! If you passed out, it was a tradition that the Jollies painted green footprints on your ass—and you did not know it until you took a shower! It was the kind of paint that didn't come off. Since Arthur was black, they painted the footprints on the back of our flight suits!

We formed many friendships that lasted throughout the war. Unfortunately, we had to call on the services of the Jolly Greens again later on. On the third morning, the gunship showed up as scheduled, but we were out cold! Jolly operations told the AC that we were unavailable at the moment.

The AC said, "Fine. You can bring them back as soon as they are able."

When we woke up at noon, the Jollies brought us back to Ubon. We both had hangovers. Arthur was on the left side, and I was on the right. We were looking out at the jungle when the damn helicopter stopped in midair! That got our attention! The flight engineer, Skip Moorhouse, went out on the sponson and tightened up a cowling bolt! In our condition, we were not expecting to be in a plane that stopped in midair; it sobered us up a bit. When we got back to Ubon, we were let off, thanked for hanging in there, and went right to the barracks to crash! I slept like a baby!

I got a little rubber duck with a quacker in the bottom for good luck on the trail. I always took it with me on my flights. I kept it in my lower right-hand zipper pocket on my flight suit. Oley got it in his mind that he was going to cut the little duck's head off! After we crossed the Fence, I would take the quacker out and silence the duck so he would not be quacking all the way down if I did have to bail out! Oley tried to get my duck many times, but I was always ready for him. Time and again, that boy tried to get my duck, but I always stopped him!

CHAPTER ELEVEN

Ladies of the NCO Club

About two weeks after I got back from R&R in the Philippines, Dick Cole, a flight engineer, and I were sitting in the club. We were scarfing beers and watching the cigarette girl. Nitnoy would walk all around with her cigarette tray, selling to the patrons.

Dick had the great idea of putting her in a Spectre party dress whenever we had our parties in the club. We went to the club manager and asked if he had any problem with us buying her a Spectre outfit. He said she could wear what she wanted. When she got off work, we took her to the Okay Hat Shop and the owner made a special Spectre dress for her. It had a black miniskirt; the black blouse had her name, aircrew wings, the Spectre emblem on her front right side, a Thai flag on her right sleeve, and an American flag on her left sleeve. She also wore a white silk dickey on her neck. It cost us about seven bucks, but she got the dress okay. She wore it when we had our next party—while working! It really did look good!

All the other girls were jealous. When Dick and I returned to the club, all fifteen wanted one! We went to the club manager and talked to him. He said he did not have any objections; if the rest of the club members wanted to make dresses for the girls on their special occasions, then so be it! We went back to the squadron, took up a collection, and had enough money to make every girl in the club a Spectre suit!

About three weeks later, we had a party at the club. All the Spectre officers attended, including the commander, but they did not know about the special dresses. When we all got to the club, the women went back to their dressing room to change into the party dresses. As they came out on the floor, Hank's band played "Ghost Riders!" The non-Spectres in the club were speechless! And the commander thought it was outstanding!

The next day, the club manager was flooded with complaints about Spectre getting special treatment. He answered it by saying that the crewmembers had bought the dresses with their own money! The club had nothing to do with it. He told the crybabies that if their squadrons wanted to spring for an individual dress for the waitresses, then they should go ahead and do so, but they never did!

The last week in June, the Fortieth ARRS sent a Jolly Green chopper to Ubon to stand ready alert. The F-4s were flying nightly missions with us; remembering 625, they stood alert for about two weeks. The enlisted men bunked with us; when we weren't flying, we were scarfing beer. One night, five of us and Skip Moorhouse, the Jolly flight engineer, got an idea that we should write words to go along with "Ghost Riders." As we got more mellowed out, we started to do just that. It took us about five hours and three cases of beer to write a passable theme song, but we finally did it. It is as follows:

Sung to "Ghost Riders in the Sky"

A young airman was working on one dark and windy night,
Upon a bench he rested as he thought about his plight.
When all at once a mighty fleet of big black birds he saw,
A-flying through the darkened skies, and up a bloody draw!
Yippie, I-eh, Yippie I-oh!
The Ghost Flyers in the sky!

The planes were black and deadly and their guns were made of steel,
Their guns were firing heavy and their sensors he could feel!
A bolt of fear went through him as they flew on through the sky,
For he saw the gunners working hard, and he heard their mournful cry.
Yippie I-eh, Yippie I-oh!
The Warlord flies again!

Their faces gaunt, their eyes were blurred, their shirts all soaked with sweat.
They're trying hard to gun them trucks, but they ain't gunned all yet.

'Cause they got to fly forever in these Southeast Asian skies,
On planes a-shooting fire, as they fly on hear their cry!
Yippie I-eh, yippie I-oh!
Spectre in the sky!

As the IO flew on by him, he heard him call his name.
If you have no fear, then volunteer to fly upon our planes!
Then airman with us you will fly these Southeast Asian skies,
A trying to gun them Gomer trucks, across these endless skies.
Yippie I-eh, yippie I-oh!
Ghost Flyers in the sky!

If you ever get in trouble, your call sign is your name.
Jolly Green will pick you up and take you home again.
So you can fly forever in these Southeast Asian skies,
With Buff standing by, Spectre cannot die!
Yippie I-eh, Yippie I-oh!
Buff is in the sky!

Through these hills and valleys we will fly forever more,
One for all and all for one until we are no more.
No Triple A can touch us as we do our deadly deed,
For we are the bravest of the brave—a very special breed!
Yippie I-eh, Yippie I-oh!
Spectre flies again!

Technical Sergeant David M. Burns, Spectre Gunner
Staff Sergeant Skip Moorhouse, Jolly Green Flight Engineer

We had it copied and tried to get Hank to sing it, but he just could not understand the words.

In July, we had another mission; we flew into South Vietnam to support the fire bases that were coming under attack. Whenever they did come under attack, they would call for fast movers (jets). The jets would come in, drop their ordnance, and haul ass. Someone in Seventh Air Force figured that we could "loiter" in the area. Whenever they called for air support, we responded if we were close by.

On one such mission, the Special Forces commander called for air support. When we arrived, he heard the engines, thought we were a regular C-130, and asked, "What are you doing here? We called for air support?"

The AC asked him what the problem was.

He said that he had a bunch of VC getting close to his wire, and they were firing mortars at him!

The AC told him not to worry. "We will take care of it; just keep your heads down."

The sensors picked up the mortar pit and the location of the VC who were preparing to attack. He put the two forward twenties on line, took out the pit, and killed most of the VC who were in the open.

The commander called and said, "What do you have up there? And where are you from?"

The AC said, "We are the Big Kahuna."

We orbited the camp for about twenty minutes, and then we left. Word got out to the Special Forces guys on the ground that there was a Big Kahuna somewhere in Southeast Asia that had awesome firepower. We started getting calls from all over South Vietnam and Cambodia, but our primary mission was the Ho Chi Minh Trail. We couldn't be everywhere at once—until we got our new aircraft.

As we got more men into the squadron—and they became qualified—we did not have to fly every night. We would have a day or two off between flights. Ron "Sweet Gin" Branson and Spectre Joe had their own gun crews, but Oley and I stayed together for a while.

When the squadron men finished their one-year tour, they had a "champagne flight." For their final flights, we would meet the aircraft, wet them down, give them a Thai garland, and then take them to Spectre East, which was a shell with a roof on it. We would have a party.

One day after spending the night at the NCO club, we got word that our new first sergeant had just checked in. The squadron clerk brought him to the NCO club and introduced him to us. He was black and built like a bodybuilder. He introduced himself as "Savage Sam." As an air policeman a few years earlier, he had gotten into it with a bad guy. The bad guy hit him in the head with a hammer, and Savage Sam had dealt with him appropriately!

He was a really good guy and always looked after "his flyers." Every week or so, something would happen in the airman's club or the NCO club, and Sam would get the report. He would sit on it for a while and then forget it.

CHAPTER TWELVE

Gunners' Hooch

One day while I was sitting in the NCO club with some of the guys, a new guy jumped all over me for not taking care of the gunners! I asked him what he was talking about.

He said, "We should have a place of our own to gather. Every time we come to the club, someone bad-mouths us. We have to bust his head—and then we get hell for it. If you are as good as you say you are, why don't you get us a place of our own?"

At first, I took offense, but after thinking about it for a couple of hours, I got an idea. By this time, the airmen up to staff sergeant had moved into a big barracks with a double deck. Building 490 had been air-conditioned for us, and we only occupied the bottom floor. I went to the squadron and asked to speak to the commander and the first shirt. I had a plan to take the last bay of the first floor, facing the street, and turn it into a "day room" for the gunners.

The commander and first shirt told me to have at it—but not to break any rules! I got the gunners together, told them what I wanted to do, asked for suggestions, and told them that this was a self-help program. We would have to pay for it out of our own pockets. We had a few people good at drawing who drew up a plan; we discussed it in detail and decided to go with it. We didn't get permission from civil engineering because we were sure they would disapprove.

I went down to the CE squadron, got a hold of the Thai supervisor, and had him meet me in the barracks. I told him what I wanted, including a bar, refrigerators, and vinyl walls. I told him it would be just between us—and I would pay for all the equipment and labor he could provide.

A few days later, he showed up, and we made a deal. The whole thing—vinyl walls, long bar, lowered ceiling with indirect lighting, electrical in all four walls, and salaries—would come to about six hundred dollars, including anything we could steal. The deal was done.

We took the last twenty feet of barracks space, placed a partition between the sleeping quarters and day room, and put in a door so we could enter from the barracks. We soundproofed it as best we could. The bar was about twelve feet long, and we wanted shelves in the bottom so we could lock up our goodies.

Every day after he and his crew got off work at CE, they came to the barracks and started work. The gunners pitched in whenever they could. Amazingly enough, the secret was kept. After about three weeks, the job was done. All we needed was furniture and a refrigerator. The vinyl paneling was brown; the lowered ceiling was just right. The Thai workers did an outstanding job. We went downtown and had two poker tables made, found some "used" furniture at a warehouse, and got two refrigerators that had been "condemned." We were almost ready to open; all we needed was the booze!

Each airman had a ration card with five cases of beer per month. A bunch of us went to the BX and bought fifteen cases of beer. We put them on ice for a day and then invited the commander and first sergeant to the grand opening. From then on, it became the hangout when we got back from flying. We could relax and talk about the missions without being attacked because of who we were.

A gunner went downtown to the Ubon Print Shop and had one hundred chit books made up in five-dollar books with twenty-five cent chits. We decided to sell beer at twenty-five cents a can until we got our money back from the construction. We also had a hundred "gunner hooch club cards" made up. Thinking they would be enough, we would sell the chit book for five dollars. The NCO IC, Master Sergeant Bob Aldernik, would keep the cash in a lockbox. An off-duty gunner would tend bar until we got enough money to hire someone.

All we needed was some music. I went to the NCO club and asked the Thai manager where he had gotten the jukebox for the club. There was a company in Ubon, but they only dealt with the officers and NCO club. I asked what would happen if the jukebox in the club broke; he said he would call the company for a replacement. I checked out the jukebox and saw that the reject button was the kind that protruded from the rear; it was very small and could be jimmied easily.

The next day, I went to the club early—when not too many people were around—and waited for my moment. I pushed the reject button all the way in and offset it so that it would remain in the hole! I told the manager that the jukebox was busted. He checked it out and saw that every time he tried to play a song, it would reject.

He called the company, and they said they would come out to replace it. They did not do any work on the boxes on site; they took them to the company. I hung around and—sure enough—the man showed up, took the old box out to his truck, and replaced it with a new one!

After he left the club, I asked if I could talk to him about "something." I had a Thai waitress translate for me. I asked what it would take for him to deliver the "broken" jukebox to the gunners' hooch.

He said it was broken, but I showed him where I had pushed the button in "by accident." I asked how much commission he got from the club from the box. When he said 20 percent, I told him I would give him 50 percent!

He asked me how much I thought the jukebox could make in a month.

I said, "About $300!"

That got his attention.

When I told him that I would guarantee $200, he said he could deliver the jukebox to my hooch for a two thousand baht ($100) "delivery fee"! He would service the box with new records as they came in every month! The deal was done, and we had the only jukebox on base in a private hooch.

As soon as I got the jukebox in the hooch, a couple of gunners sent off for "Ghost Riders" by Johnny Cash. They asked their families if they would send the record to them. We got the songs in about three weeks. Once the hooch was up and running, the gunners finally had a place to go where they could relax and let it all hang out.

CHAPTER THIRTEEN

Missions

July and August were relatively quiet months for battle damage. We continued to fly nightly missions, but the trail was really slow due to the rain and clouds. Trucks were still getting through—but nowhere as many as during the dry season. Some nights, we didn't even get shot at!

September and October got a little better; we were being asked to fly into South Vietnam on troops-in-contact (TIC) missions whenever the Special Forces asked. On these missions, we usually shot up the area surrounding the camp and dropped flares so that the SF guys could use their mortars. Whenever we were above the camp, the VC and NVA broke off the attack and vanished into the jungle. We would be given a body count of anywhere from 200 to 500, depending on the size of the attack.

In October and November, we got more gunners and other personnel into the squadron. We were due to receive six new A models with the 40mm guns. Back where the rear twenties used to be, there were two 40mm guns installed. The air force had gotten them from the navy—the same type used in World War II.

We had to add another gunner to the crew since it took two gunners to operate the the forties—one to load and one to pass the ammo. These guns enabled us to fly higher and gave us a better chance of dodging the Triple A. In addition, we got a new sensor. The "low-light-level TV" was an infrared spotlight located where the combat cameraman stood. The sensor operator of the TV could see the ground as well as during the day when he used the IR spotlight.

My fellow gunners and I were rapidly approaching our one-year tour date. We were scheduled to return to the States in December 1970. The missions began picking up when we got the new planes. Our operating area was expanded to include all of Laos, Cambodia, and Vietnam when requested. The NVA were getting more powerful anti-aircraft weapons on the trail. We had to put up with not only the 23mm and 37mm anti-aircraft guns—but also the 57mm and the 100mm guns! We could operate above the 23mm guns, but the rest of them could reach us at our new altitude. And they were guided by radar! One of our aircraft took a 37mm round in the belly of the aircraft. It blew right under the belly; shrapnel went into the booth, wounding the sensor operators. They survived, but the aircraft spent three weeks in the repair revetment.

I was flying every chance I got. Bob Aldernik was replaced as the NCOIC by Master Sergeant Jake Mercer. He took over the money box from the hooch. One day, he asked to see me in the hooch. He said that we had made too much money! We had something like $5,000, and he did not feel comfortable with that much money. We couldn't put it in the bank because too many questions would be asked.

We hired two Thai ladies to be bartenders—one in the day and one at night. We also bought two barbecue pits and had a barbecue every week. We also started buying presents for every gunner going back to the States. And we would have free-drinks night. While we only sold beer and soft drinks, nothing was said about a gunner bringing his own bottle.

Lieutenant Colonel Ken Harris was expected to take over the squadron, and I flew with him a few times. He was an outstanding officer, and I had a great deal of respect for him. Around 15 December, I just did not feel right. There was something wrong, but I did not know what it was. I felt like tearing the place apart. I started crying for no reason.

"Backdoor Sam Croft," a gunner I had gone through training with, took me to the base dispensary. The flight surgeon gave me a happy shot and put me in the hospital. When I woke up the next day, some gunners came to see me and asked what happened. I told them I didn't know; I was just out of it.

Colonel Harris came to see me and asked if I was up to coming back to the squadron.

I said, "Yes, sir!"

The flight surgeon told me I had a case of "situational reaction with symptoms of anxiety and physical fatigue, commonly called combat fatigue!"

I told him I was almost finished with flying. If I was going to get something like that, wouldn't I have gotten earlier? He said that sometimes it took months to show itself.

When I got out of the hospital, I walked from the Main Gate in Ubon down to the bridge across the Moon River. It was about four miles. When I got there, I began thinking about what had happened to me. I realized I had never expected to return home! I had it in my mind that I was going to die doing the thing I loved the most—with the men I cared about most. All of a sudden I was finished. My tour was over, and I had survived! I guess that set me off!

I felt better and returned to flying. I flew my last mission on 23 December. The Triple A was heavy, but I really felt good! I had my champagne party upon landing; it was great! All the gunners wished me well and I was thanked for the gunners' hooch.

CHAPTER FOURTEEN

Going Home

I left the squadron on 26 December, went to Bangkok, and caught the "Freedom Bird" back to Travis AFB in California. When the plane lifted off, all the people on board were cheering. I felt an unusual sadness because I was leaving. I had an overwhelming feeling that I was letting my crewmembers and the squadron down. I knew in my heart that I would be returning as soon as possible.

As soon as I landed at Travis, I called Randolph Air Force Base. I talked to Brian Morrison and asked if he could send me back to Spectre. He asked when—and I said, "Now!"

He said he didn't think my family would appreciate that. He told me to call him back in twenty minutes; he would let me know something. Those were the longest twenty minutes in my life! When I called him back, he told me the earliest I could go back was on 1 June. That was the best he could do. I told him it was okay. He told me to go on to my new duty station at Grand Forks Air Force Base in North Dakota.

When I got there, I was to tell the personnel weenies that I had a set of orders ordering me back to Southeast Asia as part of the Palace Gun program. My orders would be there when I arrived. When I finally got home, I waited a day before telling my wife about my decision to return to Southeast Asia. Needless to say, it was rough in the house for a few days. She finally agreed—if I would send her and the children to Japan to wait for me to complete my year. She is Japanese; the kids loved Japan and wanted to go to school there.

I promised her I would take them to Yokota Air Base and enroll the kids in school there.

CHAPTER FIFTEEN

Grand Forks Air Force Base

After the New Year, we drove to Grand Forks. I went to the personnel office and presented my orders. I told the staff sergeant at the desk that I would only be there for six months and that there should be a set of orders for me in his file.

He said that he had heard it all before and I asked to see the NCO in charge. A potbellied chief master sergeant came out from the back and asked what my problem was.

I told him I was reporting from Southeast Asia for duty, but I would only be there for six months since I had a set of orders returning me to the Sixteenth Special Operations Squadron on 1 June, 1971.

He said that was not possible. And even if I did have orders, he would cancel them. I was going to be "here" for three years!

I asked him if I could call Randolph Air Force Base.

He said, "Go ahead. That will not change anything."

I called Brian and told him what the chief had said.

He asked to speak with him. I only heard one side of the conversation.

After identifying himself, the chief said, "Who am I talking to? What orders? When were they sent? Palace what? By who's authority? The chief of staff? This is highly unusual! Yes, sir! I'll see that he is given a copy of his orders today!"

He handed me the phone. Morrie had settled everything; I would get a set of my orders for "personal reasons." I was going to be assigned to a fighter interceptor squadron that was going to be deactivated in a year. The chief told me to come back in the afternoon to pick up a set of my orders. In the meantime, I was to report to the 460th FIS for "temporary" duty!

I reported and went through the same thing with the first sergeant. He did not know what to do with me, but I was assigned to the weapons section and trained as a load crew chief! I took three days off to get my family settled in on-base housing. After being there for about three weeks, I had some of the enlisted men ask me about being in gunships. I told them the truth: it was very dangerous, and they had a good chance of being killed or wounded. A few of them asked if I could help them get an assignment. I told them to think it over for a few days. If they still wanted to do it, I would see what I could do. I called Morrie and told him about the possibility of getting him a few volunteers. He said to make sure they were good and properly motivated; he did not want any deadheads!

After another week, five men asked if they could volunteer for the AC-130 gunship program. After talking to them and considering them to be good men, I took their names and gave them to Morrie. He said they would be receiving a set of orders within three weeks based on "verbal volunteering." Of those five men, two would eventually be shot down, and one would be killed in action. I asked Morrie what was going on elsewhere and if he had heard from any of my friends.

Al Warmonger, Kevin Mullaney, Spectre Joe, Jerry Olson, Ron Branson, and Arthur Humphrey were scheduled to return in a few months. Six other men had asked for and received orders to return to Spectre in June and July 1971! It seemed like I was back with my flying buddies! Since I did not have their phone numbers, I asked Morrie to give my phone number to all the guys when he contacted him. These guys were everywhere—from Nevada to California to Washington! As luck would have it, they all beat me back to Ubon! Time seemed to pass very slowly, but June finally arrived.

CHAPTER SIXTEEN

Return to Spectre

On 1 June 1971, I packed up my family, put our stuff in storage, and left Travis Air Force Base. When we arrived at Yokota Air Base, I got a house for the family, enrolled the kids in school, and set up my family. I spent two weeks with them and then flew to Ubon Air Base. When I arrived, I reported to the squadron. As I was greeting the troops, Colonel Harris, the squadron commander, came over to greet me.

With a grease pencil in his hand, he said, "Welcome back, Sergeant Burns." He placed the grease pencil mark on my sideburns, which I had let grow long, and said, "Everything below the mark, shave!"

I knew I was home! Jake Mercer took me to the gunners' hooch to talk about things. The gunners had bought two more card tables, a regulation dice table had been donated by Chief Master Sergeant Cusamano, the personnel chief, and they had four versions of "Ghost Riders" on the jukebox.

Everything seemed to be going fine in the running of the hooch. I was asked to resume my management of the hooch and agreed to do so. By this time, we had received our new aircraft with the 40mm guns in the rear. We also had the new LLTV sensor installed. We had received a whole new group of gunners, and the squadron was beginning to grow in strength.

There were at least a dozen returning gunners, and they were made crew chiefs. Some were assigned to the stand evaluation section. The "stand eval" gun crew also flew with the new guys and made sure they were "combat efficient." As a returning gunner, I was given three check rides. Since I had come out of the navy to join the air force, I was familiar with the 40mm gun. It is the same gun the navy used. The only difference was that we had loaded the gun toward the sky in the navy, and it pointed down 30 degrees on the gunship.

When I heard that first *ka-thunk, ka-thunk, ka-thunk, ka-thunk* of the pilot firing the 40mm, it brought back many memories. When I completed my three check rides, I chose my own gun crew. Although Oley had an opportunity to get his own gun crew, he chose to stay with me for a while! He probably had plans for my rubber ducky.

Before the week was out, I was back in action. With the new forties, we could fly higher. This enabled us to dodge most of the Triple A, but we still had to worry about the 37mm, 57mm, and 100mm. On my second flight with a new pilot, we took a 37mm hit in the left wheel well! The shrapnel went mostly downward, but some sprayed around the inside. Luckily, no one was hit this time!

We returned to Ubon; there was some concern about the landing gear working, but we landed without trouble. Ron Branson, Arthur Humphrey, and Don B. also returned. It was so good to see these men again. I guess we all had the same idea. We would ride this war out together.

The nightly flights increased until we had three or four Spectre gunships over Laos at one time. As usual, the country was divided into areas; the gunships would operate in an assigned area unless fragged to another area to assist. The North Vietnamese and Pathet Lao were in a panic and were supplying the entire Ho Chi Minh Trail with anti-aircraft artillery. More 37mm and 57mm guns were placed around the trail, and the 80mm and 100mm guns were placed in strategic areas. Those two guns were traceless, so all we saw was the flash of the firing—and then we would have to hold our breath for a few seconds. The 37mm fired a set of seven rounds. Most of them were tracers that looked like small basketballs coming toward us. The 57mm was more like a big basketball; it seemed to rise slowly until it was near you—and then it sped up!

At the start of the dry season, the truck kills of Spectre improved dramatically! Some gunships would score in excess of twenty-five trucks damaged or destroyed on one mission. We had a TV recorder and a voice recorder installed on the plane so every kill was documented. Because of the voice recorders, we were told to keep the language clean! Every time the tape was turned on, we would say "Hello, tape. Fuck you, tape!"

We would rely primarily on the forties since they allowed us to go higher and give us more reaction times for the Triple A. There was a rumor that the NVA was starting to move SA-2 surface-to-air missiles down the trail for the specific mission of shooting down Spectre! There was one unconfirmed report of a missile being shot at Spectre, but it appeared to be unguided. We were given F-4 escorts on our missions to suppress the anti-aircraft fire. Most of our escorts were from the 497th TFS Fighter Squadron at Ubon, but other squadrons at Ubon would assist us between their daily missions to North Vietnam. Every now and then, when fighters from Ubon were not available, Moonbeam would assign a fighter from Danang, South Vietnam, as our escort. This was a severe pain in the ass because they did not know anything about gunship operations. They were lucky if they hit the ground with their bombs.

The nightly flights were taking a toll on our aircraft, and the ground crew was working twelve to fifteen hours a day to keep the gunships flying.

CHAPTER SEVENTEEN

Spectre Maintenance

The maintenance crews assigned to Spectre were just as combat-oriented as we were. They were dedicated to the mission and would willingly do anything they had to in order to keep the aircraft flying.

If it were not for the maintenance troops, Spectre would be grounded and unable to fly its missions. They were appreciated by the squadron and very well respected! The one man that any crewmember, including the aircraft commander, did not want to cross was the crew chief! He was in charge of that gunship; it was his plane—and we were only borrowing it for our missions! He kept that plane in outstanding condition. It was clean when we checked it out from him—and it better damn well be clean when we returned it to his charge! He looked after that bird like a mother hen. And when we returned it with battle damage? He wanted to know what happened. Who hurt his bird? Did we do anything about it? He took it personally, and it was like the NVA had shot him as well! He probably was the most unappreciated person in maintenance, but he was respected by the air crews! What he said about his plane went! He was the last person we saw when we left Ubon and the first we saw when we returned.

When I was not flying, I was looking after the gunners' hooch and trying to stay out of trouble. One of the ladies working at the hooch asked if she could make sandwiches and sell them to the gunners. She wanted to charge twenty-five cents apiece and would give the hooch a nickel for each sandwich. I saw nothing wrong with that and gave her permission to do so. She made all kinds of sandwiches—vegetable, meat, and Thai—and she would be sold-out before the gunners went to fly each day. She changed her schedule to have some available at night. We were doing a very good business at the hooch; we were still using the chits in order to keep out the non-Spectres. We didn't need any bad publicity or attention drawn to the hooch since I never did get official approval to build it!

We scheduled outdoor barbecues every Sunday. The lady workers and some of the gunners' girlfriends would get everything together, and I would pay them for it. We had all kinds of Thai food—pork, beef, and some things I did not even know what they were. It all tasted great!

I set it up with the NCO club manager that whenever we had a final flight party, he would reserve a part of the club for us. The girls still had their party suits and were dying to wear them. These were held about every three months, and it was not a problem for the club. There were always some people who did not want to move out of the reserved area, and we could not forcefully move them out. When the troops arrived, they got the message and voluntarily moved.

When the plane landed, the off-duty squadron personnel office and enlisted would meet the plane, drive the crew around the base on the party wagon, play "Ghost Riders," and end up in front of the club. Hank's band and the working girls made a lot of tips that night. They really looked forward to the "Spectre parties!"

Arthur Humphrey

AC-130 Gunship

AC-130 Gunship in Korea with Drag chute

AC-130 Gunship

Brian Morrison and Dave Burns

Left to right Bob Jacobs, unidentified,
Jake Brenner, Brian Morrison

Me with my Capt Spectre Cape

Dave Burns and Jerry Olson

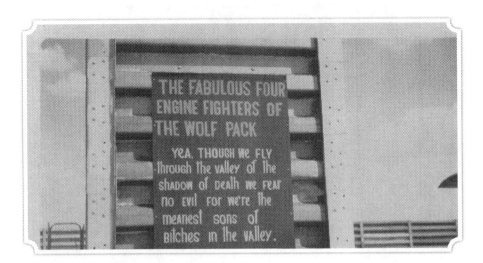

Sign on revetment

The Sockey Game

The Sockey Game

The Sockey Game

The Sockey Game

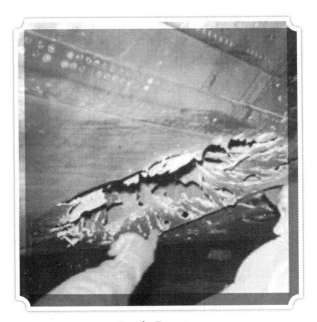

Battle Damage

Battle Damage

AC-5091

David Burns

In Formation Over Korat

In many ways, members of a modern-day phalanx

by Lt. Col. William R. Harms

Around 600 BC a new military formation came on the scene which could sweep anything else off the battlefield. Every Greek male youth who could afford the cost of armor spent long, arduous hours of practice to the beat of the drum to perfect the skills expected of each member.

The phalanx permeated the social fabric of the nation and upon its perfection hinged the deterrent strenght of the military and hence it's survival.

An AC-130 crew is much like the ancient phalanx inmany respects. Men who spend endless hours in rythmic exercises and who experience the sudden release and exhilaration of combat are marked for life. The long briefings and inspection rituals, like the dance around the fire by our proto-human, hunting pack ancestors, stir the genes normally dormant in our bodies.

Again, akin to the phalanx, where each mans shield covered the warrior alongside, each member of the crew depends on another for survival in the extra hostile environment found at low altitude and slow airspeed.

In the same way, we see conspicous feats of individual bravery as intolerable and out of place as cowardice. Unique in it's operation, in no other airborne weapon system do so many depend on the exactly coordinated efforts of each other for mission success and survival.

Spectre is proud to be part of the 388th Tactical Fighter Wing. We are proud of our past accomplishments which spur us on to excellence each time we are called upon.

We prefer a little chaos and controversy to strict symmetry and neatness of organization.

If we sometimes seem welded together in stubborness about our aircraft, it's because we are:

AC-130

Ron Branson Jeff Henderson Kevin Mullaney
Danny Hoppell Don Boudreaux

The 105 Gun

Dave Burns, the last good-bye

CHAPTER EIGHTEEN

One-in-a-Million Shot

As November 1971 began, the flights increased. It was all business; there was very little time for partying and such. The flights were four and a half hours long and each night was like a shootout at the O.K. Corral!

Some planes sustained serious battle damage, but the crews were unharmed. That changed when a gunship took a direct hit in the belly. It went into the booth and wounded the IR and BC operators. They were hit in the legs, and a gunner in the booth took shrapnel in the gut. He would have been more seriously hurt if it had not been for the combat gear he was wearing.

The next night, Bennie the Bean (the AC) was flying aircraft *628* when they took a 23mm round up through the nose gear. It bounced off the flight engineer's seat! John S. was not wounded, but the plane was down for a week for repairs.

Two nights later, my crew flew with Bennie to the Kilo area. The moon was almost full, and we were expecting a hot night from the Gomer gunners. Whenever I flew, I always loaded my .38 with tracer rounds. We were not supposed to do that, but I could not see trying to load my pistol if I had to bail out! I would have other things to do, such as pulling the rip cord!

I was flying the scanner's seat on this mission; Jerry A. was the flight engineer. The Triple A started once we entered the area, and they were trying very hard to lead us—and do us bodily harm! All of a sudden, I saw seven rounds of 37mm fire coming right at us from the three o'clock position!

I called, "Triple A. Accurate! Break Right!"

Three rounds were going under us, and three rounds were going over our wing—but one round seemed to be coming right into the scanner's window! I was looking right at it, and it was coming straight in! I pulled out my .38 and started shooting at it rapidly! All of a sudden, it detonated right off the right wing! The three rounds above us went on and detonated far above us, and the bottom three did the same thing! The forward gunner told the commander that I was shooting my .38 out the scanner's window!

I told him I thought I hit the round with my .38! The navigator said that it was impossible; after much discussion in the air and later, we reached the conclusion that the round was defective or I had managed to hit it and detonate it! The commander chose to believe the latter! To this day, I am the only gunner to get into a gunfight with a 37mm round and win!

The crew went to the hat shop and had a patch made with a cowboy boot and a set of spurs on it. Above and below the boot were the words "John Wayne Qualified!" They presented it to me at one of our parties, and I still wear it on my party suit!

The gunners on the trail were getting really good at tracking Spectre, but there was nothing we could do. We had to fly in a left-hand orbit in order to fire on the trucks. We received some new ammunition for the forties. The "mesh metal" consisted of hundreds of fleshettes that burst out red hot when the round hit the target. It would set fire to anything around it—even the rice trucks would burn! Since the rounds were in short supply, they were reserved for the aircraft on the trail.

About two weeks later, my crew was arming our aircraft—and the ammo people accidently put two cans of mesh on our plane. Since we were fragged for south Laos and Cambodia, we did not rate the new ammo. I kept it anyway. We were patrolling the road when we got an emergency call from a fire base that was under attack. They were about to be overrun! Moonbeam dispatched us to the area, and we contacted the ground controller. "Hotel Takeo" said the Gomers were in a ditch surrounding the base and were hitting him with mortars and RPGs. He did not know how long they could hold out. He asked us what we were.

The pilot said, "Don't worry about it. Just keep your head down."

After identifying where the bad guys were, we fired on them. Their cover in the ditch kept us from stopping them completely. As we orbited their site, they would try to charge the fire base when we were not in the area. I notified the pilot that we had two cans of the new ammo aboard and asked if he wanted to use it. We loaded two clips of the new ammunition into number three forty mm gun and fired on the Gomers. That did the trick; the fleshettes exploded all around the Gomers, went into the ditch, and broke their attack! We then went to the twenties and got most of them before they could completely escape!

The ground controller was ecstatic! He wanted to know who we were and where we were from so he could send us something. The pilot told him to forget it—we were glad to assist. We went back to searching the roads.

A couple of days later, I was called into the commander's office. Colonel Harris asked if I had loaded some of the restricted ammo on the aircraft a few days earlier.

I said, "No, sir. The ammo people did!"

He chewed my ass out for using the new stuff without permission. If the praise that Spectre got from Special Forces had not been so great, he would have had my butt. Instead, he dismissed me and told me to be more careful next time!

Norm Evans reported aboard from the *119* gunship. He was an old air commando vet and knew the gunships well. John Winningham, the IO, reported for his second tour. "Gentleman John" was the NCOIC of the IOs. All the younger guys looked up to him. We were flying all-out now.

The aircraft call signs changed from the alpha codes to "Spectre." The call signs became Spectre 11, Spectre 22, etc. I'm sure the North Viets and Pathet Lao appreciated this! About this time, the gunship had its first encounter with a SAM-2 missile. The Spectre was flying an armed recon mission just north of Tcehepone and was firing on three trucks.

The IO called out, "Good God! I think I saw a SAM launch! SAM at five o'clock low! Break right! Break right! It is now at six o'clock!"

The pilot immediately put the plane in a dive and turned left in an attempt to break the SAM lock on.

The IO said, "It's still coming!"

The pilot went into a rapid dive and split-S maneuver! The SAM broke lock and went chugging on by at the speed of sound! It detonated far above the gunship. The pilot pulled out of the area and called Moonbeam to report the launch. Moonbeam wanted confirmation that it was not an unguided rocket! The pilot told him that the big son of a bitch chased him all over the sky! For some reason, the pilot returned to the area, spotted more trucks, and rolled in to attack them.

The IO yelled, "Another SAM launch!"

The pilot knew how to break the beam, but he damn near bent the wings off! When the aircraft landed in Ubon, it had to be repaired and then sent to Germany for an extensive repair! He had popped some of the rivets and maybe bent the wing spar with the wild evasive maneuver! The AC-130 was not designed to get into a pissing contest with a supersonic SAM missile! And the fact that the NVA could afford to shoot two SAMS at one gunship had serious consequences for the Spectre!

All the crews were briefed on how the pilot got away, and we started to train for such an event. The Seventh Air Force seemed to think this was a onetime thing, and the gunship missions continued on the trail.

December 1971 was a great month for the Spectre gunships. The trail was dry, and the trucks were running hot and heavy. This time, we had enough gunships to cover almost all of Laos and South Vietnam. Each plane was accounting for between fifteen and twenty-five trucks per night! We were putting the big hurt on the trail, and the NVA was surely going to take more action than they had before!

Two more gunships reported SAM-2 launches and got the hell out of Dodge for the remainder of the night! The missions went on! Right after these incidents, there was a crash program to install radar-homing-and-warning (RHAW) gear on the gunships. They would pick up radar signals from the radar-equipped guns and the "Fan Song" radar used by the SAM-2.

War Story: The One-Eyed Hawk

Oley lived downtown. One day, a samlor driver brought him a sickly looking baby hawk! His right eye was infected, and the samlor wanted to sell it to Oley. Oley gave him a buck for it, cleaned it up, and fed it—but could do nothing about the eye! He tied a string to its leg, and let the hawk fly around his bungalow once in a while. Oley claimed that the one-eyed hawk could tell his fortune!

Oley once showed up at a crew briefing without his combat gear. The AC asked where his gear was.

Oley said, "I asked the one-eyed hawk if I was going to fly today. He looked at me with his good eye and shook his head."

The AC told him to get his gear anyway. When we got out to the aircraft, the crew chief said it was broken!

A couple of weeks later, Oley showed up at the briefing with all his gear—including his helmet! The AC asked Oley what the one-eyed hawk had to say about the mission.

Oley explained that the hawk said we were "going to really be shot at tonight!" During the mission, we drew more than a thousand rounds of Triple A!

About a week later, Oley showed up at the briefing in tears. He hugged Arthur, the IO, and me. He said that it had been a pleasure to fly with everyone!

The AC asked what the one-eyed hawk had to say about the mission.

Oley said, "I asked the hawk what the mission was going to be like. He rolled his good eye, looked at me, and rolled over and died!"

More than one crewmember wondered what was in store for us. In fact, Oley's girlfriend got tired of the hawk stinking up the place and tried to give it a bath! In the process, she managed to drown the hawk! We flew the mission, got six hundred rounds of Triple A, and destroyed ten trucks! So the hawk was about half-right!

CHAPTER NINETEEN

Near-Death Experience

January 1972 started off with a bang! The first three days, two Spectre flights, one operating in the Plain of Jars area and the other one operating in the Barrel Roll area reported a SAM missile fired at them. Their RHAW gear picked up the SAM activity light, the SAM tracking signal, and finally the SAM launch light! The problem was that the SAM-2 had dual capability. It could launch using the Fan Song radar or—if the moon was bright—it could launch visually, which meant we had no warning other than seeing the actual launch! Both aircraft evaded the SAMs and returned to Ubon without damage.

Even though these launches were reported to intelligence, there was no action being taken to protect the gunships other than giving us fighter escorts with hard bombs and a few HARM (high-speed, anti-radiation) missiles.

On 4 January, my new gun crew (James S., Ed R., and a new gunner) was assigned to load crew duties. This was from the time that the first aircraft returned to Ubon until the last, which was around 0600 on 5 January. On our last reload, we pulled the ammo trailer up to the ramp. Ed started to pass the 40mm clips to me. I had one foot on the trailer and one foot on the plane.

The new gunner was putting the clips into the containers on the right side of the plane. Jim S. was working on the 20mm guns forward. Ed kept stacking the 40mm clips on top of each other. I told him to slow down and pass them to me one at a time. He would do that for a while and then stack them again! I told him not to stack them because they were unstable and would drop.

He passed two clips to me one at a time. As I turned around to pass them to the new guy, Ed put two clips on the top of the can. I turned around and saw that one of the four-round clips was falling! I bent over to catch it and saw the rounds come out of the clip. One hit the ground right between my legs! The last thing I saw was a bright yellow light. I heard a big explosion, and then everything went silent! I saw myself going through a dark tunnel. There was absolutely no sound. I was traveling very fast. I felt no pain, and I saw a bright white light at the end of the tunnel! I was quickly approaching the light. I felt weightless and at peace!

All of a sudden, I slowed down and started to travel backward in the tunnel! Next thing I knew, I was on my belly on the ramp. The explosion had picked me up and thrown me over the ammo trailer. I landed on the taxiway about six feet from the aircraft! I heard the noises of F-4 fighters revving their engines for takeoff! I looked up and saw a great big black tire about a foot from my face! It was the front end of a fire truck that had been dispatched when they heard the explosion!

I heard Ed and Jim talking. Someone said, "Roll him over!"

The other one said, "No, man. He's dead!"

I rolled over on my own and looked down at my feet; my left combat boot was smoking! I still did not feel anything, but the look on Jim's face told me that something was wrong with my foot and legs!

The ambulance arrived, and I was taken to the dispensary. The doctors and the nurses cut off my clothes to look for more serious injuries. I had shrapnel wounds on my chest and face. My T-shirt was shredded, and I had a gaping hole in my left foot where a bunion had been! Other than that, I was alive! I was lucky that the doctor in charge was a specialist from Utapao Air Base who had been sent to Ubon on temporary duty.

He looked at me and said, "There is nothing here that I cannot fix! You'll be all right!"

They put me to sleep and worked on me.

When I woke up, my foot had been repaired. There was a huge bandage on it. The doctor had cut some meat off my thigh and grafted it onto my foot wound. The shrapnel in my chest and face was mostly powder burns. I was told later that when the round blew up, I was in the vortex; the deadly shrapnel went over and around me. The force of the blast blew me over the trailer, and I landed about five feet away!

The new gunner ran forward and jumped out of the scanner's window! Jim was blown inside the aircraft but not injured. The explosive ordnance disposal people told me the explosion had been "low order." The warhead did not explode—it had just been the powder in the casing! I should consider myself lucky because it had enough power to tear me apart! As if I needed to hear that!

I spent three weeks in the hospital and was finally cleared for full flying duty. The gunners came to razz me about not wearing my Captain Spectre cape! After getting out of the hospital, the first sergeant told me that Ron Branson and I had been promoted to master sergeant! We hit the club for a few "libations."

CHAPTER TWENTY

The Big Gun

In February, we received three E-model gunships! They had armor plating on the bottom and were going to be equipped with the new 105mm howitzer! This gun was amazing! It was an army 105 that was geared down to a 44-inch recoil when fired. Otherwise, on recoil, it would go out the other side of the aircraft. It replaced the number-four 40mm gun.

Three army sergeants from the First Cavalry Division were sent with the aircraft to teach the gunners how to operate the 105. My crew was one of the three crews to be taught the gun. After the army taught us, we would teach the other gunners. The army sergeants thought they would teach us the gun in a classroom orientation; however, they were not told that they would be flying with us in a combat environment to teach us the gun at the same time! To their credit they still volunteered to fly with us.

Having the 105 required us to have five gunners—one for the forward twenties, the scanner, and three for the 105. One gunner would operate the breech, one would load the gun, and one would pass the rounds. The warhead of the 105 weighed fifty-two pounds.

While the army loaded the gun with the barrel elevated, we would load it with the barrel depressed. Prior to flying our first mission, we practiced loading the weapon on the ground for a few days. The electronic whiz kids mated the gun to the onboard computer, and we were off to see Gomer!

On our first mission, we spotted five trucks on the trail. We started off firing the forties to get them stopped. When the pilot fired the 105 for the first time, the first shot got three trucks at once! What a sight! He hit one truck, and the blast got the two others. Gomer went ape! All their guns started firing blindly, hoping to get whatever was up there shooting at them!

Since we were at altitude, the 57s were not a very big threat. The the 37s could still reach us. That night, we fired ten rounds of 105; the hardest part was carrying and loading the warhead. One gunner would drop the breech, one gunner would take the warhead out of the rack, give it to the loader, and the gunner would give the brass casing, which was loaded separately. The loader would insert it, and the other gunner would close the breech, slave the gun to automatic, and the pilot would fire it when on target. This was a very serious increase in Spectre firepower, and it was just a matter of time before the North Vietnamese would come up with a countermeasure. For the time being, we had them by the balls!

The army guys were not too happy being shot at! They flew ten missions with us before they certified all three crews as qualified to teach. By that time, they had been thoroughly indoctrinated in Spectre. On their last night in the squadron, we had a party for them at the gunners' hooch and presented them with Spectre patches. They presented us with a First Cavalry Division patch since that was the outfit they were from. The squadron commander attempted to award them a set of permanent aircrew wings for flying ten combat missions, but the army put the kibosh on that. We gave them a set anyway.

After getting qualified, one E-model would fly each night with an instructor crew and a student crew for on-the-job training. Each night, the Gomer guns would become more accurate. They were using radar-controlled guns, and we had to do more evading and jinking in order to throw them off.

Throughout the first three weeks of March, the NVA gunners were using everything they had in order to try to bring a Spectre down. We received hits on the aircraft, but managed to return to base. There was no doubt that they were getting desperate! They even fired salvos of unguided rockets in hopes of maybe hitting us or causing us to leave the area.

When we returned to base, we were told that there was a big buildup at the the DMZ (demilitarized zone). The North Vietnamese were up to something! It turned out that it was the beginning of the NVA Easter Offensive against South Vietnam! During this time, Dick Cole returned to Spectre as a flight engineer. I met him at the terminal, and we went to the NCO club for some catching up! The ladies remembered him for the dresses and seemed very glad to see him! I told him the rumor about the Gomers starting an offensive, and he had heard the same thing in Bangkok!

Because he was a returnee, he did not have to go through the indoctrination. After three days, he was back to flying. It was good to have him back!

CHAPTER TWENTY-ONE

Aircraft *044*

On 29 March 1972, aircraft *044* flew off on its nightly mission to central Laos. It was a full moon; the aircraft spotted a convoy of trucks and rolled in to attack. They had an F-4 fighter escort on standby. When a SAM-2 missile was launched at the aircraft, the pilot evaded it. Two more SAMs were fired; the pilot evaded one, but the other one struck the aircraft in the belly!

The F-4 saw the gunship disappear in a ball of fire and the pieces falling to the ground. He attempted to attack the SAM site but could not locate it. The pilot thought they had used visual sighting to shoot the gunship down. There was no radio warning or contact during the evasive maneuver. There were fourteen men aboard, and none survived. Word of the incident reached the squadron, and everyone felt a deep sense of loss. We had not lost a bird since 22 April 70.

The NVA must have been getting desperate because they were moving SAM missile sites on the trail. They had used three SAMs against one Spectre! This made them vulnerable because the air force could use B-52s to saturate the trail if they suspected SAM sites! No such authorization had been given—as far as we knew. A gloom settled over the squadron; we had lost twenty-four men and only gotten one back since 1970! However, no one quit, the missions kept flying that night, and there was a beeper search—even though the F-4 pilot said that no one could have survived.

The Crew

Major Irving Ramsower II, aircraft commander
Captain Curtis Miller, copilot
Major Harry Brauner, navigator
Captain Barclay Young, fire control officer
Captain Richard Halpin, TV sensor
Captain Richard Castillo, IR sensor
Major Howard Stephenson, BC sensor
Master Sergeant Merlyn Paulson, flight engineer
Staff Sergeant James Caniford, IO (second tour)
Staff Sergeant Edward Pearce, gunner
Staff Sergeant Edward Smith Jr., gunner
Sergeant William Todd, gunner
A1C Robert Simmons, gunner
Captain Charles Wanzell III, CO

CHAPTER TWENTY-TWO

The Easter Offensive

The missions continued without interruption on the trail. We were informed that we might have to go into South Vietnam if the conditions there did not improve. On 30 March, we launched as usual, but we were still in shock about losing a plane and full crew to a SAM missile.

I was scheduled for the 0200 launch and was sitting in the gunners' hooch. At 2200, a gunner burst in and said, "We have lost another one! aircraft *570*, the E-model with the 105 aboard has been shot down! No word yet as to survivors! Two gunships in two days!"

We went down to Spectre operations to find out what had happened and if anyone survived. The following is a narrative of a recording made by another Spectre gunship in the area. It starts off with Moonbeam being informed about a possible Mayday from a Spectre gunship with the call sign "Spectre 22."

"Spectre 22, Spectre 22. Moonbeam, over?"

Ten seconds of silence.

"Moonbeam, Moonbeam, this is Spectre 22! We have a fire! We have a fire! We need all the escorts we can get! We are headed on course 270! We had one man bail out! Correction—we had two men bail out! We still have a fire on the aircraft; we have one engine shut down! (They took a direct hit on number three engine!) We are on 120 radial, heading toward channel 93" (Ubon Air Base).

Moonbeam requests the location of the two bailouts.

The pilot replies, "We will get you the information as soon as we can."

(There are three Spectre gunships in Laos at the moment; they ask if they can assist Spectre 22.)

Moonbeam asks Redbird (a B-57 bomber) that is close to Spectre 22 to assist!

"Moonbeam, Moonbeam. This is Redbird 12; we are drawing on Spectre at this time!"

Spectre 22: "Check us on our right side, Redbird! Redbird, we are coming up to 6.5" (6,500 feet).

Redbird 12: "We are about two miles from Spectre at this time!"

Spectre 22: "Tell us where we are, Redbird!"

Redbird 12: "You are coming up on the Fence in about ten minutes. You are about thirty miles from the Fence!"

Spectre 22: "I'm bailing them out right here, Redbird!"

Redbird 12: "Roger that! Mayday! Mayday! Mayday! Spectre is bailing out his people at this time! Co-ordnance 1530.6 and 10626.4!"

The pilot was the last to bail out. The IO acted as jumpmaster and waited for the pilot to come to the rear of the aircraft. As soon as they jumped, the aircraft went down in a ball of fire!

There was about a minute of silence on the tape and then the most beautiful sound in the world is heard! Beepers—so many beepers that they blocked out the transmission for about ten seconds! The *weep-weep-weep* sound means that someone has survived and is on the ground!

Then began the biggest rescue in Southeast Asian history! The air war stopped, and all available aircraft were assigned to fly protective cover on the downed crewmembers. After taking roll call, all fifteen men survived! All fifteen men! Two were deep in Gomer country, but they were all right.

The Jolly Greens from Udorn were airborne at first light; after the A1E's Sandy attack aircraft made the area safe, the Jollies started to pick up all our men. Air America picked up the gunner who bailed out first and took him to Udorn. Another Jolly picked up the copilot; he was the second man to bail out.

When we got the word that all fifteen men were rescued and were on the way back to Ubon, the squadron went ape! Three gunners and I went to the package store and bought thirty bottles of champagne! The entire squadron went down to the flight line to wait for the Jollies to bring our men home!

Soon we heard the sound of the rotors; three Jollies were coming in to land! As they landed, the first PJ off the Jolly was Wayne Fisk! Once again, he had rescued a Spectre gunner. The gunner on the stretcher had a broken leg but otherwise was in good spirits!

As each man was brought off, he was given a bottle of champagne—and the Jolly crewmembers were given one also. The morale of the squadron was astronomical! After losing a plane with all hands the day before, we had finally gotten all our men back. Bob J., one of the men I had recruited in Grand Forks, was one of the rescued. He was the gunner who had bailed out first, landing in the middle of the Gomers. Air America had gotten him out just in time!

From the flight line, everyone went to the NCO and officers' club to celebrate. The Jolly crews spent the night at Ubon and flew back to Udorn the next morning! It was a bittersweet moment; we had lost an entire crew—and all our men had been rescued the next day!

There was little time for relaxation. The North Vietnamese had launched the Easter Offensive. They had invaded South Vietnam from three directions; from the DMZ, Laos, and Cambodia. We were on alert to assist in any way we could; this was in addition to the nightly missions on the Ho Chi Minh Trail! However, we had enough aircraft to do the job this time!

The NVA was trying to take the city of An Loc; they had many tanks, and the Army of the Republic of Vietnam (ARVN) could not hold them back. Spectre was fragged to An Loc and given orders to destroy anything that moved! I was on the second mission there; the first Spectre had been in TIC and had broken up a charge by the NVA. As soon as we got on station, we saw five T-54 tanks trying to enter the town. We attacked them with the forties and destroyed all of them. The NVA had brought mobile anti-aircraft guns down with them.

It was a whole new ballgame to call Triple A in the daytime! We could still see the tracers, but it was hard to figure the trajectory! As soon as a gun came up, the F-4 escort made a run on it and destroyed it! We winchestered in an hour and had to leave the area and land at Bien Hoa in Vietnam. We landed, refueled, re-armed, and were back on station in less than two hours.

The fighting was fierce, but we held the city. We used the 20mm on the troops and the 40mm on the tanks and bunkers. We estimated that more than three hundred NVA were killed the first day! At the end of the first day, Spectre had accounted for thirteen tanks! The NVA kept on coming. Spectre covered An Loc all night. Every time the NVA would launch an attack against the ARVN, we would break it up! As long as we were in the air, the ARVN would stand and fight. If we were not around, they would bug out!

After flying seven hours and rearming twice, we went back to Ubon for a rest. The other Spectre gunships were patrolling around the DMZ, the central highlands around Quantri City, Loc Ninh, and Dong Ha. The NVA were attacking all along the central highlands, but the air force and Spectre were holding them.

The next morning, we were fragged down to Cambodia—by the Fish Hook area and the Parrots' Beak area. The NVA was coming up from that way, and we caught them in the open! The pilot used the twenties and wiped out a whole bunch of them! We did not depend on body counts; we knew we had succeeded when they stopped attacking!

Spectre was flying day and night; we managed to keep the missions going on the trail and in South Vietnam and the surrounding area. We would fire, land, re-arm, refuel—and do it all over again until relieved by another Spectre.

On 5 April, one of my gunners took sick. I picked up a spare gunner. Since he wasn't the smartest one in the pack, I used him on number-four 40mm, passing ammo. I was in the scanner's window, calling Triple A. Arthur was on the ramp, watching for Triple A. I was used to the sound of the forties firing. I could tell from the sound the guns made that they were firing steady.

I heard a *ka-pung-ping* twice; it did not sound right. I left the window and saw that the new gunner had left the deflector unpinned. The spent rounds were coming out and hitting the live ammo on the right side of the aircraft instead of going into the barrel behind the gun! I yelled for the flight engineer to take number four off the line! Then I told the pilot to pull off target! I ran back to the gun and the idiot was just looking at me! How one of those rounds did not hit the ammo rack was beyond me. If it had, we would have blown up into little pieces!

I picked up a spent brass round and hit the fool all over with it. If he hadn't been wearing his helmet, I would have put him in the hospital. I remembered what had happened to me in January; if a round had hit the ammo rack, we would have been history!

I ordered the front gunner to come back to the rear guns and had the idiot go up where I could keep an eye on him! I told the pilot what had happened, and we went back to the attack. When we landed at Ubon, the pilot told me to make sure that the asshole was never near our crew again!

I walked him into the stand eval gunner section. The stand eval gunners—Staff Sergeant Rich Nyhof, Sergeant Leon Hunt, and Sergeant Larry Lehrke—were there. Technical Sergeant Dennis Peterson, the NCOIC, was in the operations office. Each man was on his second tour with Spectre. I physically threw this dumbass gunner into the office. When I told them what had happened, they grounded him right on the spot.

I went to the operations officer and told him about the incident. He turned pale when I told him that two rounds had hit the ammo rack! He grounded him permanently and had him transferred out of the squadron to the ammo dump! It took a while for me to stop shaking! I kept thinking how all fourteen of us could have been killed due to one man's stupidity! I went to the gunners' hooch to unwind, and the asshole was there. He came up to me and asked why I was so upset! I lost it! I belted him so hard that I knocked him out the front door! In the regular air force, I suppose I could have been charged with assaulting a junior airman. In combat, I had done him a favor!

The next day, one of the Spectre gunships was hit with a heat-seeking Strela missile over An Loc. We didn't know that the NVA had them so far south. The missile hit the left rear of the plane, went right through, and detonated just as it went out the right side! Since the IO was wearing his ballistic helmet, all he got was a headache. The missile bent the rear of the plane a little sideways, and the pilot had to go back to Ubon at once! The damage was so bad that the plane had to go to Germany for a major overhaul.

The daylight missions went on all over South Vietnam wherever we were needed. While we were covering an area, it was never overrun! The Easter Offensive continued for about sixty days, but we were fragged as needed. The army choppers and the air force B-52s took care of the area.

We went back to concentrating on the trail where all the supplies were coming down to South Vietnam. The NVA were doing everything they could to stop Spectre. Our planes were being hit every night, but we always managed to return to base. The truck kills were fantastic. On one mission, the Spectre destroyed forty trucks, and it wasn't unheard of for one plane to get in excess of twenty-five trucks per mission!

All our planes had video recorders installed, and our truck kills were documented! The two remaining 105s on the E-models were natural-born tank killers! Even a near miss would cause an explosion! In May and June, I flew almost every day and night. The nighttime missions were limited to four hours, but the daytime missions—with refueling and re-arming at Bien Hoa—could last six or seven hours!

We also flew down to Cambodia to assist the Royal Khmer Armed Forces. They were in danger of being overrun by the bad guys, but as long as we were in the air around them, the bad guys could not mount an attack. Each time they tried, we would hit them with the twenties and forties! Those missions would last for about four hours before we would be relieved by another Spectre.

We were in a battle with the Gomers trying to overrun a Khmer outpost when we got a call from an American fire base. Fire Base P needed assistance. The call was for "any gunship in the area, we need assistance!"

Our orders were to respond immediately whenever we got a call for assistance from an American outfit. We had to break off the attack and go to the aid of the fire base. It took about ten minutes to get there. When we rolled in, there did not seem to be any action on the ground. The pilot contacted the FB and asked what the problem was. The ground controller told us that the FB commander (an army captain) wanted us to patrol around his base and see if any enemies were around!

Our AC said, "We thought you were under attack!"

The FB said that he had a problem because none of his men wanted to go on patrol outside the wire!

We had broken off an attack to defend the Khmers because a bunch of grunts did not want to patrol. The AC told them to defend themselves because he had work to do! We went back to the battle.

While we were gone, the good guys did take some casualties! The AC reported the incident when we returned to Ubon.

CHAPTER TWENTY-THREE

The Gunners

Jake Mercer and I were discussing the gunners' hooch. Jake was a master sergeant and a navy veteran as Kevin Mullaney and I were. We had all come over from the navy for one reason or another.

Jake asked if I was going to extend my tour.

I said I did not dare—my wife would leave me if I did.

He said I was needed here in Spectre; the young guys looked up to me. They thought that as long as Dave Burns could do it, so could they!

I took that as a compliment and told him that my heart really was in Spectre, but I wasn't ready for a divorce yet! We discussed having a party at the club to get rid of some of the money. The jukebox was doing great! There were four renditions of "Ghost Riders" on it; the most popular were by Vaughn Monroe and Johnny Cash! The jukebox owner was really pleased with the setup and was making a lot of money since the jukebox played almost twenty-four hours a day!

Oley had been promoted to technical sergeant, and the operations officer made him take his own crew. He was one of my closest friends, and we still hung around when we were off duty. He was an outstanding lead gunner! He had a good crew, and they looked up to him as a combat veteran! When Dick Cole joined the stan eval crew, the entire crew was returnees.

My rotation date was rapidly approaching. I was due to leave on 6 July. Brian Morrison was trying to arrange a transfer for me within the Pacific Air Force (Okinawa). He could work miracles and was the backbone of the enlisted gunners. He kept them out of the mundane air force bases and did his best to see they would go where they wanted. His call sign was "Spectre Protector."

I was called to the personnel office one day and told that my transfer orders were in. I had been assigned to the Eighteenth Tactical Fighter Wing at Kadena Air Base in Okinawa on a command-sponsored tour! Morrie had come through! At that time, telephone calls were hard to come by. I sent a letter to thank him. I brought him up-to-date on what was happening with the gunners he had sent over and the knucklehead who had almost gotten us killed! He put his name in the "never send book." He was quite concerned about the safety of the men he sent over. He took it personally when something happened to them.

I was talking to the crew in the stan eval office. All of them, including the NCOIC (Dennis P.) were returnees. They were discussing whether they should extend their tours en masse or singularly. Rich Nyhof asked if I was also going to extend. We had gone through gunner school and snake school together in 1969. I told him that my wife damn near killed me because I came back this time!

He said, "That sounds like a personal problem!"

We shot the breeze for a while. Rich, Larry, and Leon had motorcycles. Whenever they were off duty, they went out to the Ubon countryside to ride. They were planning a short trip in July if the flight schedule permitted. Jake Mercer took a group of gunners to the BX to buy more beer for the hooch.

Oley came in, and we went to the club. When we got there, we saw a group of gunners shooting the bull. Spectre Joe was there and half-ripped as usual. He had an on-and-off-again thing going with one of the waitresses. Moose was currently involved with the air police sergeant.

She said, "Joe! I have a new bed that my Teelock bought me!"

Joe said, "Let's go try it out!"

They left the club together. They came back about an hour later, and Moose went back to work. About thirty minutes later, the AP sergeant walked in the club with a few friends. Joe saw him and called him over.

The boy did not like Spectre, and it showed in the way he walked over. Joe looked him in the eye and said, "Sarge, that is one fine bed you got for Moose! Nice and soft!"

I damn near choked on my beer!

The staff sergeant said, "What the hell do you mean?"

When Moose saw what was happening, she came right over and attempted to take the AP from our table. He was about to bust Joe's lip!

Joe said, "Dave, that asshole is going to hit me! Are you going to stand for that?"

I said, "Boy! You are on your own!"

I wasn't going to let that big son of a bitch hit him, but Joe did not know that!

Moose finally got the AP away from us. As she left, she looked at Joe and said, "Joe, you sumbitch!"

Joe just smiled his evil smile! We decided to go to the hooch since things were getting dicey at the club! The AP was beside himself that a Spectre troop had backdoored him while he was working!

That sort of thing happened a lot, but we had never bragged about it before!

CHAPTER TWENTY-FOUR

Aircraft 043

On 18 June 1972, the stand eval crew was scheduled to fly a mission to the Ashau Valley. This was a nightly occurrence, and it turned out that it was this crew's turn to go.

Since Dennis P., the gun crew chief, was scheduled to give a check ride to another gunner, Jake Mercer took his position. Six of the enlisted men were on their second tour. They took off from Ubon at 1745. They entered the Ashau Valley and immediately found three trucks parked on the road. They rolled in to attack, and the IO reported Triple A coming up from the eleven o'clock position.

Dick Cole, the flight engineer, said, "No threat."

They picked up about fifteen more rounds of 37mm fire. They were attacking and avoiding the AAA fire when Bill P. saw a large white flash on the ground at the six o'clock position.

He yelled, "Strela, Strela. Six o'clock! Break right!"

The student IO, Staff Sergeant Donald Klinke, launched a flare. The missile seemed to hone in on the flare, and then it broke lock and hit the number-three engine! There was a white roaring flame down the right side of the plane; it was so bright that it lit up the inside of the aircraft! The plane seemed to level off for a few seconds, and then it started a small roll to the left! The pilot rang the bailout bell.

Bill P. did not have his chute on, but he had it in his hands. When he looked back, he saw the gunners holding onto the 40mm guns. The plane exploded; the right wing fell off and threw Bill P. and two of the officers in the booth out of the plane! The officers had backpacks and pulled their ripcords at once! As Bill was falling, he hooked his chute up to one side of his harness and pulled the ripcord! As he was dangling by one strap, he saw the plane break into four pieces. He saw four distinct flames on the ground. He hit the trees on landing and turned on his beeper. The Jollies and Sandies were overhead within the hour. Bill and the two officers were picked up and brought back to Ubon at sunrise.

At 1945, we got word that another Spectre had been shot down! As usual, we gathered in Spectre operations to await word on the number of survivors. We were told that there were only three beepers that checked in, but the rescue effort was underway.

It was daylight before we got the men back, and they immediately went into a briefing so we could not talk to them. We had just lost the most experienced air crew in the squadron; six of the enlisted men were on their second tour! I was devastated. The crew was experienced and should have survived that shoot down.

I made up my mind that I was going to avenge them and stay in the war as long as it took—no matter what. Morale hit bottom; all we could think of was to get back to the valley to do a beeper check. The Ashau Valley was crawling with NVA; anyone who survived and was taken prisoner would probably be kept alive as bargaining chips. If they fell into the hands of the Pathet Lao, they would have to shoot it out. The Pathet Lao did not take any prisoners—especially gunship crewmembers!

The Crew

Major Robert Harrison, navigator
Major Gerald Ayers, IR sensor
Captain Mark Danielson, BC sensor
Staff Sergeant Richard Cole, flight engineer (second tour)
Staff Sergeant Donald Klinke, IO student
Master Sergeant Jacob Mercer, aerial gunner
Staff Sergeant Larry Newman, aerial gunner
Staff Sergeant Richard Nyhof, aerial gunner (second tour)
Sergeant Leon Hunt, aerial gunner (second tour)
Sergeant Stanley Lehrke, aerial gunner (second tour)
Captain Paul Gilbert, aircraft commander
Captain Robert Wilson, copilot

On 19 June, my aircrew (Captain Tom Sietzler was the aircraft commander) was assigned to patrol the Ashau Valley, do an armed reconnaissance, and listen for beepers. We took off from Ubon at 1800 and entered the valley at about 1845. We were given strict orders from the operations officer not to descend below 10,000 feet during the mission. We were not to go into the valley unless all our equipment was operational.

As we entered the valley, the IO said that the flare launcher control box was not working. I told the pilot that I would take responsibility to manually launch the flares if they were needed. We were desperate to get into the valley to check for beepers! After some discussion the pilot agreed, and we proceeded to the area.

An F-4 from the 497th TFS at Ubon was above us on the lookout for Triple A or missiles! We were in the valley for about forty-five minutes. At the assigned altitude, we were not getting any hits on the trucks we were shooting at. When the pilot decided to go lower, we spotted three trucks and went in to the attack. We were firing on the trucks and on our third orbit when the flight engineer saw something.

Staff Sergeant Jack Davis yelled, "Strela! Strela! Break right! Break right!"

The pilot immediately broke the aircraft in a 95-degree, 2G bank and said, "Get that flare out!"

I was violently thrown against the flare launcher. I reached out and grabbed the firing handle with my right hand. I heard the *kaboom* as the flare was launched, and my right wrist became numb. As I struck the launcher on my right side, I felt a pain in my chest. I felt like I had broken something.

The missile came up from the eleven o'clock position. It was guiding on the second engine when it broke lock and hit the flare I had launched. It went off about fifteen feet behind the aircraft and lit up the inside of the aircraft when it exploded! I saw the explosion and felt the heat! It took less than ten seconds! I felt we were out of control and tried to put on my chute with my left hand.

My fellow gunner said, "Dave, help me!" John W. had been thrown to the right side of the aircraft and was pinned there by g-forces.

I reached down with my good hand, picked him up by his harness, and braced him against the door. I was attempting to hook up his chute when the pilot rolled out of his bank! The F-4 had observed where the Strela had come from and dived in to attack. He dropped all his bombs on the site! There was no doubt that this was the same son of a bitch who had brought down *Aircraft 043* and my friends the night before! We immediately left the area, and the pilot reported to ABCCC that we had been shot at by a Strela and had injured aboard. John W. had a pain in his back. Another gunner had fallen on his knees and could not get up or walk. I could not breathe properly and suspected I had broken a rib or two. And my right wrist was useless.

This missile attack was identical to the one the night before, but we had beaten it! The pilot declared an emergency, telling Ubon we had injured aboard. When we landed, the ambulance met the aircraft and took us to the dispensary. John was bruised up badly, but nothing was broken. The other gunner may have fractured his kneecaps. I had a broken wrist and two broken ribs, but we were alive!

On our way back to Ubon, I had time to reflect on what had happened. I realized why we had so few survivors when our aircraft were shot down. We were such a close-knit crew and thought so much of each other that no one was going to leave a fellow crewmember behind if he could help it. I had thought that we were out of control. I could have jumped—I had one ring hooked up to my harness—but as soon as I heard John call for help, all thoughts of jumping became out of the question! If we had been out of control, we would have all gone in together. There was no time to think about yourself. There was no fear—only concern for a friend! I believe that attitude had prevailed in the aircraft we lost. Those men were as close to me as my family—and closer in some cases! There is no doubt that all of us would have been KIA if the pilot had not been able to evade the missile. The pilot was too busy trying to get control of the aircraft, and we were busy trying to hold on to think of ourselves!

The doctor put a cast on my wrist, taped my ribs, and grounded me for three weeks. It was 19 June, and I was scheduled to leave for Okinawa on 5 July! I knew that I had to fly one more time or I would regret it for the rest of my life.

The next day, the operations officer called me into his office and told me to have a seat. I knew something was up! He knew I was on my second tour and already had over 287 missions. He asked if there was anything I wanted to tell him about the "mission."

I told him as much as I knew.

He asked me our altitude.

I said, "Colonel, I have no idea. You know the gunners have no way to know that."

He said, "That's true, but you have been there before. What is your best guess?"

I said, "Whatever the aircraft commander says. He would know better than I would."

He suspected that the pilot had disregarded his orders and descended below 10,000 feet.

I told him I would not know about that. All I could say was that we were doing our duty, and we owed our lives to his flying ability!

He dismissed me, and nothing further was ever said about that!

The nightly flights went on, but there were not to be any more flights into the Ashau Valley during the full moon! We could fight the SAM-2, which was radar-guided or visually guided, but the Strela was visual! The only way we knew it was out there was when we saw it launch. Captain Tom told the other pilots about his radical movement and suggested they do the same if possible.

Being grounded, I had to take over the books from Jake Mercer. He had all the money and books in his locker. Things were really grim around the squadron for the next couple of weeks. The fact that they had been shot down and we survived was a topic of much discussion. I preferred to think of it publically as the luck of the draw. Many questions were asked, and a few opinions were offered. The main thing I told the gunners was to be extra vigilant! Take nothing for granted and make sure that every man was at his station! I recommended that no aircrew training be done in a high-threat area or during a full moon! There was not enough time to talk anyone through a procedure when hell was coming up at supersonic speed!

Time passed very slowly for me, and I began to have nightmares about *625*. I could not get over the fact that my friends were gone! I envisioned them all falling from the aircraft without parachutes as the plane exploded and broke apart! It must have been a horrible death! None of them had their chutes on because of the g-forces associated with the wing falling off.

I went outside and cried my eyes out for a few nights. I never discussed it with anyone else! It was too painful to talk about. I had served with these men for over two years! I had to figure out a way to get back to flying! I felt that I was letting the gunners down by leaving! I did not want to go. I wanted to stay and finish the fight, but I would lose my family if I did. And I was preparing myself for just that!

Each time I went to the doctor, he told me to wait. On 2 July, I cut the cast off my wrist, went down to the ops officer, and told him I had been cleared for flying. He asked where the paperwork was, and I told him it was in my locker.

The next night, I joined my crew and flew into the Iron Triangle! I had the heebie-jeebies until takeoff; after the wheels were up, everything was fine! On my last mission of 1972; we destroyed seven trucks, dodged three hundred rounds of Triple A, and came back alive! When I landed, the party wagon met me for my champagne flight. We went to the NCO club, had a party, and then went to the gunners' hooch.

The next day, I had a hangover. The operations officer asked me where my clearance was. I told him I would bring it to him in the afternoon. I went to the flight surgeon and told him what I had done. After much discussion about my family lineage, he cleared me for flying and backdated it a day. I delivered it to the operations officer.

I was called into the squadron commander's office and informed that I was being recommended for the Silver Star and Purple Heart for my actions on 19 June! On 5 July, the gunners had a going-away party for me downtown!

Bill W. (Worm) presented me with the 40mm casing that had blown up in January. He had collected all the pieces, taken them downtown, and had them chromed and put in a glass case! He called it "The Order of No Purple Heart."

CHAPTER TWENTY-FIVE

Leaving

On 6 July, a group of gunners escorted me to the airport so that I could catch the plane to Bangkok. I had a horrible feeling that I was doing something terrible by leaving them behind! Every sense of my body told me to stay. I didn't want to leave them, but I had to go!

If I had extended for six months, my orders would have been canceled. God knows where I would have ended up. As I got ready to board the plane, I looked at each of them and felt ever so proud to have served with the bravest, most dedicated bunch of young men in the air force! They knew that each night they flew, they may not come back. The NVA was getting a lot better at shooting at them, yet they did not quit! They continued to fly together—and help one another—whenever they could. Each man was vigilant and did his duty!

I realized that—come hell or high water—I would be back! I fully understood what that would mean to my family, but there was nothing else I could do! I boarded the plane and flew to Bangkok. The next morning, I boarded an Air America 737 from Bangkok to Yokota Air Base. I had the middle seat; there was an airman by the window and a captain in the aisle seat. I fell asleep with my seatbelt loosely buckled—it had become a habit over the years.

All of a sudden, I was flying the trail. Arthur was the IO, and we were under attack. The plane was hit in the right wing, and the pilot rang the bailout bell! Arthur was on the ramp, and I was trying to reach him—but I could not get to him.

He kept yelling, "Come on, Dave! Take my hand! We got to go!"

I tried my best, but I could not reach him! I said, "Wait for me, Arthur. I'm coming!"

"Hurry up! We're going to crash!"

I gave it a really hard try but could not reach his hand! I finally said, "Go without me, Arthur. I've had it!"

He went over the side—and I woke up! I had the airman at the window pushed down in his seat and the captain almost out of his seat! If I hadn't had my seatbelt fastened, I would probably have jumped clean out of the seat! I was sweating, my heart was beating a hundred times a minute, and I was breathless! The airman looked scared, but the captain was a fighter jock. He said, "Must have been one hell of a dream!"

I was embarrassed when the captain said I was calling Arthur's name. I got up and went to the head to wash my face!

When I landed in Yokota, I took a cab home. I was glad to be back with my family and alive, but I was still thinking about Spectre in the back of my mind. At night, I would imagine what the guys were doing, what area they were flying in, and how their missions were going.

After three days, I went to the base and called Morrie by military line. He was glad to hear from me. I told him I was in Japan, but I wanted to be back in Ubon! He could not help me directly because I was in Pacific Air Forces now. He had a few friends he could contact and told me to call him back in a few weeks.

I got the family ready to go to Okinawa. We had to be there in three weeks. After a week, I called Morrie, and he gave me the name of a master sergeant to call in Hawaii when I got settled. They were good friends, and the master sergeant would work something out for me.

CHAPTER TWENTY-SIX

Arriving in Okinawa

I reported to the Eighteenth Munitions Maintenance Squadron at Kadena Okinawa for duty. When I walked in, the chief master sergeant said, "That's all I need—another master sergeant!"

I told him I would be glad to go back to my old outfit if he would sign the papers; as usual, he was full of crap! All mouth no action!

I got into off-base housing, enrolled my kids in school, and tried to settle down and be a normal human being. I wasn't too successful at it! After a month, I called the master sergeant at Hawaii, introduced myself, and told him my status.

The best he could do was cancel my long tour (three years) and assign me a short tour (eighteen months). After that, he could transfer me back to the Sixteenth SOS. It would be up to me in order to keep current in my flying physical.

I told him that if that was the best he could do, then it was all right with me. Another month passed before my orders were amended to eighteen months. By this time, I had talked to my wife—and the writing was on the wall! If I went back, she was gone!

In October, I received my orders to report to the Sixteenth SOS in December under the Palace Gun program! When my orders came in, I was summoned to the commander's office. The commander was a lieutenant colonel who had never been in combat, and he was interested in my assignment.

I told him I was bound by the secrecy act. All I could say was that I had been in the Sixteenth for two years, and our missions were classified. After sweet-talking him for an hour, I conned him into sending me back to Ubon every ninety days to stay current. He would give me fourteen days permissive TDY orders. I spent most of my time signing safety reports in the office, and going to the NCO club. It was a practice to go to the club for happy hour and then go home half-drunk! It was a daily occurrence with most of the NCOs, but I could not handle it on a regular basis. My mind kept going back to Ubon and the people I had left over there.

On 11 December, the commander gave me my first set of permissive TDY orders for Ubon under the heading "Training." I went to the SAC terminal; they had daily KC-135 refueling tankers going to Utapao Air Base in Thailand. Once there, I would take a taxi to Bangkok and then a train to Ubon! I checked into the gunners' section after checking in with the first sergeant. I was welcomed back and spent a good number of hours in the gunners' hooch.

Bob Elliot, the gunner I had recruited in Grand Forks, was doing fine and thinking about extending his tour. He had matured since I had last seen him. He had filled out and was looking good. The commander would not let me fly since I did not have flight orders, but I was brought up to date on the 105 and missions and safety procedures.

John Winningham and I went downtown a few times. He was on his second tour and was scheduled to go home soon. We talked a lot about the squadron, the new guys, and the officers. He said they were good—but not as aggressive as the original bunch! The anti-aircraft fire on the trail was really accurate now, and they were uneasy descending below 10,000 feet. With the 105 and the forties, that was okay, but in order to use the twenties, we had to descend to 7,000 feet.

The squadron was flying into Cambodia and South Vietnam more regularly. Everyone wanted a Spectre overhead! I told him about coming back for a third tour. He said he would like to, but it was not likely.

CHAPTER TWENTY-SEVEN

Another Loss

On 21 December, *490* departed Ubon at 0540 on a combat mission. They were attacking three trucks. At about 1910, the pilot descended to 7,500 feet for some unexplained reason. He was firing the twenties for about half an orbit when the gunship was hit in the wing root by a 37mm round!

The aircraft pulled out of orbit and was attempting to go back to Ubon. Fuel was flowing into the cargo compartment, and it was about sole-deep on the floor. John Winningham, the IO, had two gunners on the ramp with their chutes on. He was the most experienced crewmember on board—he was on his second tour—and he knew just how dangerous the situation was!

The plane was flyable, but it was very dangerous with the fuel sloshing around on the floor. The electronic equipment was still turned on, and the slightest spark would be disastrous! The plane flew on for about ten minutes; there was no panic from the crew, and everyone was at their stations.

Someone from the cockpit called back to the booth and asked for the aircraft manuals. John grabbed them and started up to the cockpit—and the plane exploded! It veered hard left, and the compartment filled with flames. The lead gunner (Willy) and another gunner had been on the ramp with John; they were blown over the side. Bob Elliott was in the scanner's window and probably didn't have a chance.

The escorting F-4 saw it break into three pieces. Out of a crew of sixteen, only two survived what should have been a controlled bailout situation! No one will ever know what was on the pilot's mind by keeping the crew on the aircraft when the cargo compartment was sole-deep in fuel!

There have been opinions stated by officers and enlisted crewmembers of the squadron, but what's done is done. Nothing good could come from stating them here. It falls under the fog of war!

The Crew

Captain Harry Laggerwall, pilot
Captain Stanley Kroboth, copilot
Captain Thomas Hart III, navigator
Captain Robert Liles Jr., fire control
Second Lt George Macdonald, TV sensor
Major Paul Meder, IR sensor
Captain Delma Dickens, IR sensor
Captain Joel Birch, BC sensor
Technical Sergeant James Fuller, flight engineer
Technical Sergeant John Winningham, IO
Sergeant Robert Elliott, gunner
A1C Charles Fenter, gunner
A1C Rollie Reaid, gunner
Major Francis Walsh Jr., ACM

This was the sixth aircraft we had lost since 1969—and it was not getting any easier to handle! Even though the squadron was huge, getting an aircraft shot down was still devastating!

Winningham and Elliott were the two crewmen I had known longest. I felt responsible for losing Bob—even though he had volunteered and knew the risks involved.

I could only imagine what Brian Morrison was feeling! Every gunner that was sent over there had been sent by him! The men in Hickam Air Force Base in Hawaii said he was a sensitive, caring human being and was a professional NCO who took things like this personally! I truly knew how he felt! Losing six aircraft and fifty-four crewmen was a severe loss for a squadron this size! The war was not over yet—and there was no idea when it would be over!

After the memorial service, I went back to Okinawa and assumed my normal duties. I halfway settled into the squadron, but I was returning to

Spectre in the back of my mind. My wife wanted to go back to Japan and wait out the year there. I began to make plans for the move.

On August 15, the Spectre flew its last combat mission in Vietnam! It seemed the war was all but over in Vietnam, but there was still a little dustup in Laos and Cambodia! My orders were still good; the squadron had not gotten any word of leaving.

My time in Okinawa was spent doing mundane things; the commander knew I had special orders and did not want to put me in any position of authority.

I went back to the Sixteenth two more times. Each time, it was harder to leave. The squadron was flying all out and killing trucks left and right! They were also getting their share of battle damage, but we did not lose another aircraft.

CHAPTER TWENTY-EIGHT

Return to Ubon

During the last week of November 1973, I took leave and relocated my family to Yokota. I got them squared away and left for Ubon. I flew a World Airways contract flight from Yokota to Bangkok. When I got to Bangkok, I called the gunners' section and told them I would be in the next morning on a direct flight from Bangkok.

When I arrived, I was met by Kevin and a group of old and new guys at the plane. They brought the party wagon for me and took me to the squadron. I met the commander, and Kevin took me to CBPO (central base personnel office) to officially check in.

They had a new building; as I entered, I saw a row of tables in front with a bunch of seats taking up the floor space. There were about thirty people waiting to process in. I told Kevin that I probably would be there for a while. He just smiled!

A master sergeant came out of the office and called for Master Sergeant Dave Burns to report to the office. As I approached him, I noticed his nametag—it was Brian Morrison! He had gotten himself stationed in Ubon! He stuck his hand out to shake my hand.

I said, "We will have none of that shit!" I gave him a big hug! After all this time, I had come face-to-face with the man who had taken care of me since 1969! The three of us went to the club. He told one of his airmen to process my records and said we would be back "sometime."

When we got to the club, I asked how he had arranged his transfer. He said he could do anything—and I believed him. He had to come over and watch over his "boys" to make sure they did not get in trouble! A name for him came to mind; from that day on, he was known as "Spectre

Protector!" We stayed in the club for two hours and then went back to personnel.

In the morning, I went to the squadron, officially checked in, and got my flying gear and personal equipment. As a returnee, I was already qualified. The operations officer decided to make me a floating gunner for a while. I would fly with different crews and observe how the gunners did things.

He asked if I wanted to be assigned to the stand eval section. I politely refused, preferring to have my own gun crew. When I went to the awards and decorations section to check in, one of the officers found my record from my prior tour and asked if I had gotten my awards yet. I told him I hadn't seen or heard of any. He told me I had been put in for the Silver Star and Purple Heart in 1972! About three weeks later, he called and said the Seventh Air Force had lost the award recommendation, but Colonel Hopingardner was resubmitting the paperwork.

I checked out the gunners' hooch. It was still looking good and making money hand over fist. They still had the chits—and there were three women working there. We had twenty-four-hour coverage.

We were flying night reconnaissance missions around the border of Thailand and down to Cambodia. There was still fighting going on, but we were not officially involved in shooting unless shot at. We had radio contact with the ground forces and would tell them where the bad guys were.

When not flying night missions, we were flying daytime training missions in southern Thailand. I talked to the commander and asked if it would be possible to have Brian Morrison fly a mission with us. At first, he was against it—but I told him about Morrie's dedication to finding the best people for the squadron from 1969 on. After pleading with him, he finally gave his approval!

I waited until the full moon to inform Morrie that he was approved for a mission. At first, he didn't believe me, but we did not get his commander's approval. We gave him a two-hour crash course on survival gear, bail-out procedures, how to hook up his chest chute, and what to do if he landed in a tree!

When we took off for the mission, we put him in the scanner's window so he could look out in the jungle. Off in the distance, we could see shooting and explosions because the Cambodians and Laotians were still fighting! We gave him a tour of the airplane. He saw how the sensors worked and got a look at the ground with the TV sensor!

We flew a four-hour mission. I could tell he was really excited to be flying with us! We took him up to the flight deck so he could see how they operated up there. When we landed, the gunners met us at the aircraft with the party wagon and drove to the Spectre hooch for a little libation! As the new guy, he had to buy a round!

Joe was getting ready to rotate to the States again, but as soon as he got back, he would request to come back! Most of the old-timers had been assigned back in the United States. The new guys were just as dedicated as the old ones; the only difference was that they were not being shot at nightly!

We were flying a lot of training missions down in Utapao. Most of our missions were over water, and we would have target practice in the ocean. We would throw out a flare marker and shoot at it. We would also practice breaking away from simulated Triple A.

From the scanner's window, I would yell, "Triple A, three o'clock, accurate! Break right!"

The pilot would do a lazy right break! I called him on the interphone and told him that he might as well go back to Ubon because he had been shot down! I told him with that lazy-ass right break, he would have been hit with all seven of the 37mm rounds! I told him that break right meant just that! Break right! Not some half-ass Lazy Susan!

The boy was a newbie and took offense! I reminded him of the break my pilot had done on 19 June 1972. He had immediately broken right in a 95-degree bank at 2G negative after being told to by the flight engineer—and we had evaded the missile! That was the kind of break he had better get used to if he hoped to survive the next shooting war.

When we landed, the pilot reported me to the operations officer.

The officer said, "Well? What's the problem? You had better start listening to your crew—especially the combat veterans. They will save your ass one day—if you are lucky!"

Then he dismissed him!

In March 1973, Oley returned! He had became bored with the States and decided to bless us with his presence! Ron Branson was also scheduled to return!

CHAPTER TWENTY-NINE

Korea

In April, Seventh Air Force decided to send two AC-130 gunships to Korea for a five-day firepower demonstration. They were sending one A-model with the forties and one H-model with the 105 gun. The squadron commander would be piloting one and a marine major—who was an exchange pilot—would take the other one. The commander wanted gunners who had been in combat to go since they were the most experienced.

My crew was chosen to go on the A-model with the marine major. I took three combat-tested crewmembers and two new crewmembers. The H-model crew was the same. As we prepared to leave Ubon, the IO "borrowed" an F-4 drag chute to use on our arrival in Osan Air Base in Korea. Since Osan had never seen a gunship, he wanted to deploy the drag chute when we landed. We did not tell the major for obvious reasons! His idea was to tie the drag chute to the ramp and throw out the canopy after we slowed down on landing.

As we landed in Osan, the IO threw out the drag chute.

The control tower said, "Good chute, Spectre!"

Major Mullins came on interphone and said, "Okay, gunners. What do you do now?"

When we pulled into the aircraft parking spot, we rolled up the chute and put it in the aircraft. Everyone, including the commander, got a kick out of that—except the F-4 people at Ubon who discovered that one of their chutes was missing.

Once we were assigned to our barracks area, we went to the NCO club, which was open on a twenty-four basis. Officers and enlisted went there since we were in our flight suits with no rank insignias.

The next morning, we were briefed on our duties. The aircraft would take off at the same time, and we would fly to the range, which was named "Nightmare" and perform for the dignitaries on the ground. There were old trucks and fifty-five-gallon drums on the range. Our mission was to destroy them with as little shooting as possible.

The H-model performed first, and the gunners were so fast that there were actually three 105 rounds hitting the ground one after the other! One round hit the ground, one round was in the air, and one round was being fired. The audience was most impressed! When our turn came, we put both twenties and one forty on the line! It was an amazing sight to see!

After we landed, the maintenance troops we had taken along had to replace the barrels on the twenties. The Koreans were so impressed that they wanted to buy the aircraft right then and there. When we were not flying, we were being entertained by the Koreans. There were three generals and some other ranks; they wined and dined us every night.

After flying the day missions, we went to the NCO club as a crew and had a few libations. They always had dancing girls on a stage. After watching them for a few minutes, we sent drinks backstage. It didn't take them long to unwind, and a good time was had by all!

At the end of the five-day demonstration, the Koreans threw a party for us. When we returned to Ubon, the commander gave us a couple of days off to recuperate.

CHAPTER THIRTY

Korat

In May, we got word that we were going to be relocated to Korat Royal Thai Air Base in July as part of the American drawdown in Southeast Asia. Ubon Air Base was closing as far as the US Air Force was concerned. The girls at the NCO club wanted us to have a final party. They wanted to wear their party suits one more time, and we obliged them! The advance team left for Korat in June to prepare the way for our move. Our reputation had preceded us to Korat! When the advance team got there, the NCO club manager banned "Ghost Riders" from being played in the club!

When our departure day arrived, it was a sad occasion. Spectre had been in Ubon since 1968, and we had lost all our aircraft and crewmembers there. We really did not want to leave, but orders were orders. I would come to miss the people. They were always very friendly to us. The bar girls just packed their bags and moved to Korat with us! The air force found jobs for the NCO and officer club staff in the other bases in Thailand if they wanted them.

We flew into Korat in four-plane formation—right over the base! And as we landed, the advance party had the party wagon on the flight line blaring "Ghost Riders." As the planes were put to bed, the air and ground crews went to the assigned barracks. The two-story barracks were a lot like the one we had in Ubon. The aircrew barracks were air-conditioned, which made things easier. Korat was in the middle of the country, and it could get very hot in the summertime! Our operations building was bigger than the one at Ubon, and all our offices were in one location.

We had two days off before flight operations began, and we took advantage of it. We invited the squadron commander to the NCO club.

As we sat there, someone asked the band to play "Ghost Riders." The band leader said he could not do it because of the club manager. The commander asked to see the club manager and after a "private" conversation, "Ghost Riders" was played! From then on, we did not have any trouble with the manager.

The training flights from Korat to the Gulf of Thailand were much shorter than from Ubon. We spent most of our training flights over the ocean. The senior NCO quarters—technical sergeant and above—were off to one side. There were two-man rooms with a lounge/day room in each section. I was assigned a single room since I was a master sergeant.

One day, I was sitting in the gunners' section. The office clerk brought a new gunner into the office. It was Gene Fields! He had managed to convince the air force to return him to Spectre for another tour. As he was a returnee, the first shirt assigned him to my room! We had started out in the Bat Cave as bunkmates and now—after four years—we were together again. After a lot of clapping and hugging, I took him around the squadron and introduced him to all the squadron members. He was quite a celebrity, and the new guys stood in awe of him! The squadron commander and operations officer kidnapped him. They went into their offices and had a long conversation. It lasted for over an hour. Then we went to the club to unwind. We got off into a corner with a couple of other second-tour personnel.

His story was pretty much as I had heard, but he did say that Major Brooks knew they had been fatally hit and remained in his seat and rode the plane in with complete control until the end. He saw the plane hit; it looked as if Major Brooks just glided it in for a landing! The tail end was engulfed with flames, and he heard the ammo cooking off from his chute. His burns healed well, and he spent over a year in the hospital. He was then given an assignment near his home. I took him back to the squadron so he could finish checking in.

A few days later, I ran into a PJ from NKP who was at Korat on standby. I asked if he knew what had happened to Wayne Fisk. He said that Wayne was at NKP. He was on a return tour like the rest of us. I got his phone number and planned a surprise for him.

I called him and, after all the "glad-to-be-back" talk, I asked when he was coming to Korat. He said that now he knew I was there and Spectre was there, he would be down in a week. I didn't say anything about Gene; I was going to wait until he arrived.

When Wayne arrived, I took him to the NCO hooch, got him a beer, and told him I would be right back. I woke Gene up and told him to come with me because I had someone I wanted him to meet. When he walked into the hooch, Wayne took one look at him—and there was not a dry eye in the place! After about four hours of drinking and telling war stories, Wayne had to go back to the PJ hooch. After his tour in NKP, he had been assigned to the Philippines and then worked his way back to Thailand.

A week later, Morrie called from Ubon and said he was going to come down to visit with us for a while. We met the aircraft; when he got off, he had an awful lot of luggage! We asked how long he planned to stay.

He said, "Oh, about a year or two!"

He had worked himself a transfer to Korat to look after his men! He did not know about Gene Fields. When we took him to the club, Gene was there. We told Morrie that we had someone who wanted to meet him. When Gene introduced himself, I thought Morrie was going to faint! He had tried to find out how seriously Gene had been wounded back in 1970, but the air force would not tell him anything! Those two guys hugged each other and must have talked for over an hour before anyone else could speak! Wayne had met Morrie in Ubon and was very glad to see that he was in Korat.

After that, Wayne would hang out with us whenever he was in Korat. In October, Ron "Sweet Gin" Branson returned—and so did Kevin Mullaney! It seemed that we had all the combat veterans coming back—but no combat to fight! At least not yet. We still took off with a full load of ammo on our training missions. The rumors were hot and heavy about the South Vietnamese and ARVN troops not holding their own and the possibility of being overrun. Nixon had promised to come to their aid, but after he stepped on his dick, it seemed the politicians didn't have it in them to help the South Vietnamese government.

Even though we were officially out of the war, anything was possible—and the squadron maintained 100-percent combat capability! I finally got my awards for the action of 19 June 1972. The Silver Star was downgraded by the Seventh Air Force to the Distinguished Flying Cross for "heroism," and I got the Purple Heart. Seventh Air Force had cut and run after 15 August 1973. There was just a skeleton crew there. They were all ground-pounders, and no one knew or cared what was going on. I put them in a box with the rest of my decorations and forgot about them.

The gunners got together and decided to build another gunners' hooch like the one we had in Ubon. This time, I knew who to contact. I went hunting for an interpreter! I found a sweet thing and went to the civil engineer squadron to look up the Thai boss man! I made him the same deal about using his labor force, and he made me a deal: he would provide all the necessary equipment for an additional fee! There was no need for me to scrounge around for wood and paneling because he had all of it in his area!

The air force didn't know or care what was there. I got together six hundred dollars, cleared it with the commander (verbally), and they began work as soon as they finished their normal shifts. Within three weeks, the hooch was up and running! It was beautiful inside! It had wall paneling and recessed lighting on the walls! It was a really professional job! The money was well spent! We had brought most everything from the old hooch, and there was very little to buy! We brought the refrigerators, the poker tables, and the tape recorder.

I had to go downtown to get the jukebox. The boss man said he could get me one, but he wanted 50 percent of the take! After looking like I was having a heart attack, I agreed! All we were interested in was the music. When the jukebox guy in Ubon picked up his jukebox, one of the gunners took all the records—including "Ghost Riders"—and brought them to Korat. We were in business again! Each unit in Korat had a "day room," and our hooch went under the radar! Two of the girls who were with us in Ubon followed us to Korat, and I rehired them! A third one was the girlfriend of one of the returnee gunners!

The squadron had continued to expand until we had over five hundred assigned personnel! We had more than 130 gunners! We had sixteen aircraft and were flying on patrol and recon training missions every day and night. We had a four-day R&R every month; most of the old-timers would hire a bus to take us to Bangkok. We stayed at the Metro Hotel, where we used to stay whenever we were in Bangkok. The hotel staff catered to us, and we could do almost anything we wanted to do there.

A few of the old-timers were married to Thai women and had commissary privileges. They would hire the hotel van and go shopping! They would load up on all sorts of American stuff, put it on top of the bus, and carry it back to Korat! As time passed in Korat, we became acceptable to most of the base. We would hold monthly parties at different places downtown courtesy of the profits we made from the gunners' hooch. The flight engineers had their own small hooch in the NCO section, and they would have Sunday barbecues of mostly pork chops and buffalo steak.

Colonel Hopingardner, the commander, completed his tour of duty and was replaced by Colonel James Wyatt. He turned out to be an outstanding squadron commander as Colonel Hopingardner had been. Spectre was very lucky in that respect. All our commanders were flyers and had a flyer's mentality. Look out for your men, take care of them—and they will take care of you!

In wartime, we were exempt from the peacetime inspections the air force just loved to hit the squadrons with. They started coming around with a vengeance. Spectre passed everyone without one discrepancy! The flying and administration inspections were passed with outstanding ratings!

In October, the flight engineers decided to have another barbecue. They bought the pork and steak downtown and left it out overnight—without refrigeration! That was a no-no in the Thai weather. They had a ball on Sunday afternoon; by Sunday night, most of them had come down with stomach poisoning! That was very bad for the squadron; we did not have enough engineers for Monday's missions! After that, the squadron commander banned all pork from the NCO hooch without first checking it out!

Two weeks later, the engineers walked a live pig through the main gate! The air police were dumfounded; this had not happened before. They wanted to ban the porker from coming on base, but they were not smart enough to contact the hospital. The flight engineers brought the porker to the NCO hooch, had the Thai ladies and workers butcher it, and we had "fresh" pork on the hoof! The commander pretended to be pissed, but privately he laughed his butt off! This time, there was no stomach poisoning!

In November, I received my orders to an air force base in Louisiana! I immediately called Morrie and had him meet me at the hooch. He had not seen the orders yet. I asked him if I could somehow get out of the assignment. He told me the only way he could help me was for me to "voluntarily" extend my tour in Spectre for another year! If the squadron commander would go along with it, Morrie would handle the paperwork.

We went to see Colonel Wyatt. I told him that Spectre was my home, and I did not want to leave it as long as it was in Southeast Asia. He asked about my family, and I told him I could take care of that. He thought about it for about a minute and then told Morrie that if I volunteered to extend for a year, he would approve it! So the deal was done! I had another year with the squadron and people I loved. I would be doing what I loved doing! Two weeks later, my original orders were canceled. I was safe for another year! All I had to do was tell my wife! I requested leave and went to Japan to see her and the kids. She wasn't completely surprised, but she liked Japan. The kids were getting a good education through the military schools. She told me to do as I saw fit, but the writing was on the wall! I returned to the squadron and resumed normal day-to-day activities.

On New Year's Eve, we had a squadron party at a place called Vena's Farm! It was out of the way, and we hired a bus to take the people from the base to the party and back for those who wanted to return that night. The next day, we resumed flights over Cambodia. The whole area was falling apart! Without American air support, the Cambodians and South Vietnamese were hurting. We did leave enough aircraft in Vietnam for them to defend themselves, but their hearts seemed not to be in it. By 1 April 1975, the Khmer Rouge had taken all of Cambodia except for the Phnom Penh area. The royals were fighting as best they could, but they were doomed without ammunition or air support!

CHAPTER THIRTY-ONE

Fall of Saigon/Phnom Penh

On 11 April, the squadron was alerted to an upcoming mission that was classified. It would start at about 0600 on 12 April and continue until "further notice." It would be a combat mission with a full load of ammo.

At 0400, the first two aircrews were briefed. The mission was to fly close air support around the US Embassy in Phnom Penh, Cambodia, as part of operation "Eagle Pull." At 0600, they were over the embassy, and the marine helicopters from the ships at sea started the evacuation of Cambodia! Although the Khmers were just outside the city, there was no anti-aircraft fire and the evacuation went smoothly. By nightfall, all our planes were back in Korat! It was a sad situation; we had been helping the Cambodians since 1971. They were willing to fight, but did not have the ammo or air cover anymore! Things were quiet around the squadron the next day, and we were wondering when the South Vietnamese would collapse!

On 28 April, we got our answer! Once again, Spectre was going to fly a combat mission—this time in support of Operation Frequent Wind! The evacuation of Saigon was going to be hairy since the North Vietnamese were outside the city and advancing! On 29 April at sunrise, two gunships were dispatched to the Saigon area to fly close air support around the US Embassy. The evacuation was chaos on the ground! The ARVN had cut and ran; they were trying to get out of Saigon anyway they could. They were armed and were pushing the civilians aside. If we had to fire, it would be difficult to tell the bad guys from the good guys! Fortunately, we didn't have to do any shooting. The mere presence of the gunships overhead held the NVA off! The evacuation was completed on 30 April. Now the only free country in Southeast Asia was Thailand!

I did not fly on Operation Frequent Wind. Morrie and I spent the time in the gunners' hooch with Morrie playing "Sweet Surrender" on the jukebox. It was a really traumatic time. After all the missions and aircraft and aircrews lost, the NVA had won! Although we had never lost a battle, they had won the war because of the corruption in Vietnam and the idiots in the United States! It was something we had not thought about during the war, but now it came to the forefront!

After the fall of Saigon, we were assigned to fly cover for Operation Eagle Pull. For the evacuation of Phnom Penh, we flew cover over the soccer field while the embassy staff evacuated. It was nowhere as chaotic as Saigon, and the bad guys did not fire on us. There was no need for any more recon missions. From then on, we flew the Thai border between Cambodia and Laos and kept the Thai military informed of any and all traffic coming into the country.

If we saw small sapper teams crossing the Mekong, we informed the border patrol of their location—and they wiped them out! The Thais took no prisoners! Their motto was, "If you come to Thailand to do harm, you will be buried in Thailand!" A couple of teams made it as far as Ubon Province and did some damage before being killed. The traffic from Cambodia was not as much as Laos. Route 9 came from Vietnam all the way across Laos—right up to the Thai border. That was where most of the traffic was.

After Vietnam and Cambodia fell, the Thais were really nervous. Their two closest neighbors were in communist hands. They did not know what those countries had in store for them—or what the United States would do if the war started in Thailand! The United States talked big, but actions speak louder than words. They had just seen two US allies fall to the communists! We flew constantly, but we were forbidden to fire unless fired upon.

On 4 May, a group of us took advantage of the monthly four-day R&R to go to the Metro Hotel in Bangkok. We chartered a bus as usual. In the Metro, the reception desk is on the left side and the restaurant is straight back from the front door. On our second night, a group of us in the restaurant had a party. We were listening to the band that played there on a regular basis.

One of the new gunners had picked up a sweet thing; instead of bringing her to the restaurant, he took her directly to his room on the second floor. He gave her a hundred baht (five dollars) for a short time and was ready to get it on when she said she preferred to give him oral sex!

He said no thanks; he wanted the normal kind. She was insistent, and when he took off her clothes, he noticed that something was not right! She had on a tight G-string! He reached down to check it out and discovered that she was a he! She was a lady boy!

He threw her on the bed and said, "I paid for it, and I am going to get it!" The lady boy grabbed her clothes and beat feet out of the room at supersonic speed! The gunner was right on her heels! All he had on was his boxer shorts, and all she was wearing was the G-string! She ran down the stairs and out through the lobby with the gunner right behind.

He yelled, "Come back here! I paid for it, and I'm going to get it!" The lady boy's eyes were big; all she wanted was to get away! As they passed the restaurant, the place got really still for about five seconds! Even the hotel staff was speechless! All of a sudden the place erupted in catcalls!

The gunners yelled, "Don't let her get away! Get some brown eye!"

The lady boy hit the street—almost naked—and disappeared!

The gunner was left standing in the hotel doorway with just his boxers on! After he realized what had happened, he ran back to his room and did not come down until the next morning!

I laughed so hard that I pissed my pants! And the hotel staff, which was used to our behavior, also laughed!

When we got back to Korat, we told the story to all who would listen. And the gunner became known as "Speedy Gonzales, the Brown Eye Hunter!"

CHAPTER THIRTY-TWO

The *Mayaguez*

On 12 May at about 1500, the squadron was alerted for a possible combat mission! The aircrews were assembled in the briefing room and informed that the Khmer Rouge had hijacked a US merchant ship!

The first three crews were alerted for flight and told to stand by for further orders. My crew was the third crew. At about 0600 on 13 May, an Air Force F-111 spotted the ship anchored about a mile and a half off Koh Tang Island.

The first crew took off with orders to patrol around the ship and not let any boat leave the ship for the island. We were not to fire unless fired upon. The AC-130 was charged with round-the-clock surveillance of the ship. The first gunship flew the early flight, the second gunship the afternoon flight, and we had the night flight. When we got there, we observed gunboats shuttling between the ship and the cove on the island.

We were directed to fire warning shots across the bow of the boats to keep them from getting to the island. The gunboats were armed, and one of them fired at us. That was all the pilot needed. I was working the fourth 40mm gun, and we fired a four-round clip at the boat and sunk it. There is no sound on earth like a forty firing! *Ka-thunk! Ka-thunk! Ka-thunk!* We were back in the saddle again!

From then on, Spectre would patrol at night, and the fast movers would fly around in the daytime. On the night of 14 May, Spectre returned to the island and sunk and damaged several more patrol boats! We were back in action doing what we did best! The word from Washington was to seize the *Mayaguez* and recover the crew—period!

Since the Seventh Air Force was still too far away, the marines were airlifted into Utapao Air Base and the Jolly Green HH-53 helicopters from Udorn were charged with landing the marines on Koh Tang. While this was being planned, Prime Minister Kukrit Pramoj absolutely forbade the American forces from launching any action against Koh Tang from Thai soil! He also said we could not use Utapao Airfield for any air activities! In the fifties, Kukrit Pramoj played the prime minister of a fictitious land called Sarkan opposite Marlon Brando in *The Ugly American*. The American military ignored him, and we launched and recovered from Utapao.

In the predawn hours of 15 May, eight HH-53's Jolly Greens with full marine complement in combat gear landed on Koh Tang. The Cambodians let them land then opened fire on the choppers damaging all of them and shooting two of them down. They managed to offload the marines without any casualties, and the battle began! The marines established a beachhead and began firing on the bad guys. The Jolly Greens tried to support the marine casualties as best they could, but they were sitting ducks in hover mode. They tried to land on the beach but were shot up so badly they had to pull off. The fast movers from the Seventh Fleet and air force were overhead, but they were ineffective.

Spectre appeared overhead and fired right on the bad guys! The Jollies resumed their offloads of marines and ammunition. The battle raged all day until the White House ordered the evacuation from the island. It turned out that the civilian crew of the *Mayaguez* was not even on the island. They were brought back to the ship by the Cambodians. The evacuation was easier said than done! There were 230 marines on the island, and the HH-53 helicopters were so shot up that they had trouble flying. However, with Spectre overhead, they managed to evacuate all the marines—or so they thought.

Wayne Fisk came in on *Knife 51,* a Jolly. He was firing his mini guns at the bad guys. With Spectre covering, *Knife 51* landed and rescued twenty-seven marines. Wayne, ignoring the darkness and hostile fire, ran off the helicopter and across the beach into the tree line to look for any marines who may have been left behind! Fisk found two marines covering fire; with Spectre laying down covering fire overhead, he took them to the helicopter. All three returned safely, and Wayne Fisk became the last living warrior to leave Koh Tang!

As soon as they took off, Spectre let loose with all its firepower in the jungle. The firing on the helicopters stopped. Wayne had landed three times at Koh Tang, and his chopper looked like Swiss cheese. But due to the skill of the pilot and heroism of the whole crew, they accomplished their mission! We finally got a chance to pay Wayne back for him rescuing our air crews! *Knife 51* landed on the USS *Coral Sea* and offloaded the marines. Their chopper was so badly damaged that they had to get it repaired before they could return to base.

A week later, we were informed that the navy had received three distress signals from Koh Tang; it seems that the marines had inadvertently left a machine gun crew (three men) behind. The Cambodians captured and executed them before the marines could react! We returned to Utapao Air Base, refueled, and returned to Korat!

The next day, the Thai newspapers were full of reports that air force and marine personnel had used Thailand as an attack base against Koh Tang—despite the prime minister forbidding it! This resulted in a weeklong demonstration against the United States. They ripped down the sign for the US Embassy, and the Thai police had to protect the embassy personnel. Kukrit was ranting on TV about how the United States had violated Thai sovereignty. He ordered all American forces to leave Thailand immediately! We were getting ready to leave anyway; it was no big deal—but they did interfere with our monthly R&R to Bangkok!

The following week, Wayne came to visit us; he had been dispatched to Korat in the event that we came under attack. We had a hell of a party downtown and congratulated Wayne on being the last man off the island. Keeping with his modesty, he suggested that we kiss his ring and buy him a few drinks!

Although there were demonstrations in Bangkok and a few other cities, there were none in Korat. Some of the Thai communists attempted to cause a demonstration, but the people of Korat held a counterdemonstration; it turned violent and the commies got their asses whipped! The police attempted to halfheartedly break it up, but the bad guys beat feet out of there and went back to Bangkok! The whole Koh Tang thing lasted from 12 May to 15 May 1975. That was the last time Spectre fired its guns in Southeast Asia for a few years!

Even though the prime minister had ordered American forces out of Thailand, he did not seem in any hurry to enforce the order. After all, he was the last domino standing! Vietnam, Laos, and Cambodia had fallen to the communists, but the die was cast. It was just a matter of time before we would be leaving.

Each night, we still flew recon missions along the Thai border. There were border crossings by the communists, but they were not crossing in strength. It was mostly small sapper teams attacking Thai bases along the border. We kept the border patrol notified of all movements that we saw, and they handled the problems very well. Their motto—No prisoners!—was in effect.

CHAPTER THIRTY-THREE

Don F. (DC)

Don F. got sick in July and was going to be transferred to Utapao Air Base Hospital for treatment. While he was in the dispensary awaiting air travel, we went to see him and convinced the nurse to let him out for a couple of hours so we could take him to the "squadron."

She made us promise we would not give him anything to drink! No alcohol! We took him to the gunners' hooch and had a few! Wayne was at the gunners' hooch with us. With all the laughing and storytelling, time flew by. All of a sudden, we were late! We had been in the hooch for three hours, and Don was drunk as a skunk! Wayne took his jeep to his Jolly, picked up a stretcher, and returned to the hooch. We strapped Don into the stretcher, and six men carried him down the middle of the street. Morrie was in the front, reading passages from *God's Little Acre*. The people who saw us just laughed!

As we approached the dispensary, the nurse came out, looked at us, and said, "You assholes were supposed to keep him sober!" We saluted smartly, and the medics took him inside! Don later told us that she had busted a gut laughing as soon as we staggered away!

About three weeks, Don returned fit for duty. Things at the squadron were normal—daily training flights and partying at night. In July, Morrie informed the squadron that it had been alerted to transfer en masse to Hurlburt Field in Florida! So far, it was on standby, but the move would start in the next three or four months. Advanced notice was given in order for all the personnel to make plans.

I sat Morrie down, bought him a beer, and told him it was a bribe! I asked if he could work his magic one more time and get me to Okinawa for duty! I did not want to go to Florida. I had a bad feeling about my personal life. He said he would try but could not guarantee anything.

Things were slow and routine for the next few months. The people who had Thai sweethearts were getting married and putting in the necessary papers to take them to Florida.

In September, I was called to the personnel office. Morrie had gotten me my transfer to Okinawa! I was to leave the squadron for the very last time in November! I thanked him profusely and promised him free drinks for the next lifetime!

The squadron officers got together and tried to get all the names of the personnel who had served in Spectre since 1968 in order to start a Spectre Association once they returned to the United States. Spectre had been born in Ubon in 1968, so this was the first time the whole outfit would be going home. They also wanted to start yearly reunions. Morrie was a great help in getting most of the names.

I informed my wife that we were going back to Okinawa in November for a three-year tour.

She said she would talk to me when I got home.

CHAPTER THIRTY-FOUR

Leaving Spectre/Thailand

The first aircraft to leave Thailand were the A-model gunships with the 40mm guns. They left for Florida three planes at a time. There was no telling how long it would take them since they had to refuel numerous times in order to get there.

Once things slowed down and the daily routine became somewhat normal, there was time to think about all the pain and misery the men of Spectre had suffered. We had started the squadron with six aircraft and lost six aircraft! We now had sixteen aircraft and would be able to handle any future wars. And there would always be future wars. We had lost fifty-one men from 1969 to 1972. I could see their faces and remember every one of their names.

In twenty-plus years, I had never served with a more dedicated, outstanding group of men. There was something truly special about men who fly together, live together, and face mortal danger together—and do it every night over jungle terrain with no hope of surviving if you are shot down. They were truly a sight to behold.

On 10 November, the gunners had a going-away party for me; they jokingly said they were tired of having going-away parties and welcome-back parties! I told them I was really going, but I would see them again in the States for the reunions. It was a very sad moment for me. I had been with some of these guys for four years—and I was leaving for good. I'm not ashamed to say I shed a tear or two at the party.

After the party, I had a long talk with Morrie. I told him how much I appreciated everything he had done for me—and that I was indebted to him for life. I asked when he was leaving, and he said he had arranged to leave when all of the gunners were gone. He was arranging for all of them to be flown out by commercial air. He said, "My boys ain't going out on some C-141! They are going out in style!" He was true to his words.

On 12 November, I was escorted to the airport by a bunch of gunners and put on the plane to Bangkok. It was a tearful farewell. On one hand, I had always felt in my heart that I would die in combat, and now I was leaving! I had fulfilled my pledge to remain until the end. I was in a daze.

On 13 November, I boarded a C-141 from Bangkok to Yokota. Three hours later, I was home. I felt very strange being back. I loved my kids and was very glad to see them again, but I sensed there would be a problem with my wife. I told everyone to get ready to go to Okinawa. I had two weeks of leave, and we needed to get there as soon as possible.

Later that night, my wife told me she was not going. She was filing for divorce; I was going to take the kids with me. I did not fight it.

I said, "Do what you have to do."

Of course it was very hard for the kids. David was just turning fifteen, and Cathy was fourteen. I promised them that they could come back to Japan whenever possible to visit their mother.

I reported to the 418th Munitions Maintenance squadron at Kadena Air Base on 25 November. I checked in and told the squadron commander I was reporting as a single parent! I had two kids with me. He told me to take some time off and get settled in. I had so much overseas time that I became immediately eligible for on-base housing. I was assigned a house at Naha Air Base. I enrolled the kids in school, got my furniture squared away, took care of all the necessary paperwork, and reported for duty.

Since I was a single parent, the commander asked if I wanted to be the supervisor of the 20mm gun shop on the mid-shift. I told him I would appreciate that. I could get the kids off to school, get some rest, and be home when they got home. I could go to work when they went to bed.

On 10 December, I got a call from the squadron commander. He wanted to see me before I went home. I reported to his office, and he gave me an air force dispatch from the 388th TFW in Korat! The message was from Morrie and read as follows:

To: Master Sergeant D.M. Burns Subj: Aircraft Disposition, ACFT Five Seven Six off at zero seven three one local, 9 December,

> *75. Flag transferred with last acft. Your services may be required to provide corona harvest Input, As we did it our way! s/B.P.M.!*

The commander asked me what corona harvest input was, but I told him it was classified! He didn't ask me anything else!

Morrie had told me in military language that the final Spectre gunship had left Thailand!

As soon as I got into my car, I broke down! I must have cried for ten minutes in private. I used to think that it was unmanly to cry—but that was before we lost our first crew! I took leave from Kadena and flew to Fort Walton Beach in Florida to attend the first annual reunion. It was scheduled in October 1976 and has been that way ever since. All the gunners had settled in, had their families with them, and were getting back to normal.

In 1977, I married a girl I had known in Thailand. The kids didn't say anything, but I knew they did not approve. They blamed me for the divorce, and they were right! I let my love of flying in combat interfere with my responsibilities as a father. I accept that blame, and I have to live with it as best I can.

In June 1978, I retired from the air force. We left Okinawa and went to Travis Air Force Base for processing.

Epilogue

I bought a home in Vacaville, California, and went to work for the United States Postal Service. In 1984, a group of us went back to Ubon to see what had become of the place. It was beautiful! The people were just as friendly, and some of them remembered us.

When I returned to California, I ran into the aircraft commander I had flown with on 19 June 1972. He was with Major Tonto. He asked if I had gotten the award he had submitted for me. I told him that the squadron commander had to resubmit it when I returned to the squadron and that the air force had downgraded the Silver Star to the Distinguished Flying Cross for Heroism. He took offense at that and re-recommended me for the Medal of Honor for saving the lives of fourteen crewmembers and a valuable gunship!

The air force soon replied that the time lapse was too long. The air force felt I had been properly recognized for my actions! I don't always agree with the air force, but that time I did. The fact that I had saved fourteen lives, watched these outstanding men grow up, get married, and have children and grandchildren was more than enough reward for me!

In 1999, after working for the postal service for twenty years and nine days, I retired as a maintenance operations supervisor, EAS-16. My wife and I sold our home and moved to Ubon on a permanent basis. I attended the Spectre reunions every year or so and watched as the young men grew into old men with lives of their own!

We built a home in Warin Chamrap, a small town across the bridge from Ubon. My bedroom balcony faces Laos and the Mekong River. At night, especially when the full moon is up, I often sit alone and think of my brothers. I feel closer to them now than I did in the States.

My Western religion wants to believe that God has taken care of them and granted them eternal peace, and my Asian religion (Buddhism) hopes they have been reborn as noble, great men who have been blessed with happiness and wealth.

CONCLUSION

In addition to the fifty-one men lost in combat, over the years I have lost more than fifty-nine dear friends to illness and other causes. Oley, Ron Branson, Kevin Mullaney, Arthur Humphrey, Bob Dexter, Dan Hoppel, Andy Glover, Ed Rogers, Jim Thrasher, Colonel James Wyatt, Lieutenant Colonel Ken Wilson (The Gray Fox), Lieutenant Colonel Sam Schism, Lieutenant Colonel Francis Riopel (Hoppy the Pilot), Colonel Dickie Dyer, Lieutenant Colonel James West (the first president of the Spectre association), and all the others are sorely missed.

This country has been blessed to have men such as these serving the nation. And I am most humble—and blessed—to have served with them. I do think and hope that one day I will see them and serve with them again, but I am not in a hurry to do so! There are many more Spectre men still motivating others, and the squadron is still actively defending the country and the men who fight.